EPHESIANS

ABINGDON NEW TESTAMENT COMMENTARIES

EPHESIANS

PHEME PERKINS

Abingdon Press
Nashville

ABINGDON NEW TESTAMENT COMMENTARIES:

EPHESIANS

Copyright © 1997 by Abingdon Press

This book is printed on recycled, acid-free, elemental-chlorine–free paper.

ISBN 0-687-05699-3

Cataloging-in-Publication Data is available from the Library of Congress.

Scripture quotations, unless otherwise indicated, are from the New Revised Standard Version Bible, copyright © 1989, by the Division of Christian Education of the National Council of the Churches of Christ in the United States of America.

Scripture quotations noted AT are the author's translation.

97 98 99 00 01 02 03 04 05 06 — 10 9 8 7 6 5 4 3 2 1

MANUFACTURED IN THE UNITED STATES OF AMERICA

To George W. MacRae, SJ
for "the one that got away"

CONTENTS

FOREWORD

The *Abingdon New Testament Commentaries* series provides compact, critical commentaries on the writings of the New Testament. These commentaries are written with special attention to the needs and interests of theological students, but they will also be useful for students in upper-level college or university settings, as well as for pastors and other church leaders. In addition to providing basic information about the New Testament texts and insights into their meanings, these commentaries are intended to exemplify the tasks and procedures of careful, critical biblical exegesis.

The authors who have contributed to this series come from a wide range of ecclesiastical affiliations and confessional stances. All are seasoned, respected scholars and experienced classroom teachers. They take full account of the most important current scholarship and secondary literature, but do not attempt to summarize that literature or to engage in technical academic debate. Their fundamental concern is to analyze the literary, socio-historical, theological, and ethical dimensions of the biblical texts themselves. Although all of the commentaries in this series have been written on the basis of the Greek texts, the authors do not presuppose any knowledge of the biblical languages on the part of the reader. When some awareness of a grammatical, syntactical, or philological issue is necessary for an adequate understanding of a particular text, they explain the matter clearly and concisely.

The introduction of each volume ordinarily includes subdivisions dealing with the *key issues* addressed and/or raised by the New Testament writing under consideration; its *literary genre, structure, and character;* its *occasion and situational context,* including its wider social, historical, and religious contexts; and its *theological and ethical significance* within these several contexts.

In each volume, the *commentary* is organized according to literary units rather than verse by verse. Generally, each of these units is the subject of three types of analysis. First, the *literary analysis* attends to the unit's genre, most important stylistic features, and overall structure. Second, the *exegetical analysis* considers the aim and leading ideas of the unit, deals with any especially important textual variants, and discusses the meanings of important words, phrases, and images. It also takes note of the particular historical and social situations of the writer and original readers, and of the wider cultural and religious contexts of the book as a whole. Finally, the *theological and ethical analysis* discusses the theological and ethical matters with which the unit deals or to which it points, focusing on the theological and ethical significance of the text within its original setting.

Each volume also includes a *select bibliography,* thereby providing guidance to other major commentaries and important scholarly works, and a brief *subject index.* The New Revised Standard Version of the Bible is the principal translation of reference for the series, but the authors draw on all of the major modern English versions, and when necessary provide their own original translations of difficult terms or phrases.

The fundamental aim of this series will have been attained if readers are assisted, not only to understand more about the origins, character, and meaning of the New Testament writings, but also to enter into their own informed and critical engagement with the texts themselves.

Victor Paul Furnish
General Editor

LIST OF ABBREVIATIONS

1Q28b	*Rule of the Blessings* (Qumran Cave 1)
1QH	*Thanksgiving Hymns* (Qumran Cave 1)
1QM	*War Scroll* (Qumran Cave 1)
1QpHab	*Pesher on Habakkuk* (Qumran Cave 1)
1QpPs	*Pesher on Psalms* (Qumran Cave 1)
1QS	*Rule of the Community* (Qumran Cave 1)
1QSb	Appendix B (*Blessings*) to 1QS
4Q298	*Cryptic A: Words of the Sage to the Sons of Dawn* (Qumran Cave 4)
4Q416	*Sapiential Work A^b* (Qumran Cave 4)
4Q521	*Messianic Apocalypse* (Qumran Cave 4)
4QMMT	*Halakhic Letter* (Qumran Cave 4)
1 Apol.	Justin Martyr, *First Apology*
1 Enoch	Ethiopic *Book of Enoch*
2 Apoc. Bar.	Syriac *Apocalypse of Baruch*
2 Clem.	*Second Clement*
2 Enoch	Slavonic *Book of Enoch*
AB	Anchor Bible
ABD	D. N. Freedman (ed.), *Anchor Bible Dictionary*
AnBib	Analecta biblica
Ant.	Josephus, *The Antiquities of the Jews*
Apoc. Adam	*Apocalypse of Adam*
Apoc. Mos.	*Apocalypse of Moses*
Ap. John	*Apocryphon of John*
Arist.	*Epistle of Aristeas*
Ascen. Is.	*Ascension of Isaiah*
Bib	*Biblica*

C. Apion	Josephus, *Against Apion*
CBQ	*Catholic Biblical Quarterly*
CD	Cairo text of the *Damascus Document*
Cher.	Philo, *The Cherubim*
Conf. Ling.	Philo, *On the Confusion of Tongues*
Confes.	Augustine, *Confessions*
Const. Sap.	Seneca, *On the Constancy of the Wise Man*
Cyrop.	Xenophon, *The Education of Cyrus*
Decal.	Philo, *On the Decalogue*
Dial. Mort.	Lucian of Antioch, *Dialogues on Death*
Dial. Trypho	Justin Martyr, *Dialogue with Trypho*
Exeg. Soul	*Exegesis on the Soul*
Fac.	Plutarch, *On the Face in the Moon*
FRLANT	Forschungen zur Religion und Literatur des Alten und Neuen Testaments
Gig.	Philo, *The Giants*
Gos. Phil.	*Gospel of Philip*
Gos. Truth	*Gospel of Truth*
HDR	Harvard Dissertations in Religion
Heres	Philo, *Who is the Heir of Divine Things?*
Herm. Sim.	*Hermas, Similitude(s)*
HNT	Handbuch zum Neuen Testament
HTKNT	Herders theologischer Kommentar zum Neuen Testament
HTR	*Harvard Theological Review*
Hyp. Arch.	*Hypostasis of the Archons*
Ira	Seneca, *On Anger* (in *Moral Essays*)
Jos.	Philo, *On Joseph*
Jub.	*Jubliees*
JSNT	*Journal for the Study of the New Testament*
JSNTSup	Journal for the Study of the New Testament—Supplement Series
Leg. All.	Philo, *Allegorical Interpretaion of the Laws*
LXX	Septuagint
Nat. Deor.	Cicero, *On the Nature of the Gods*
N.E.	Aristotle, *Nichomachean Ethics*
Nom.	Philo, *On the Change of Names*

NovT	*Novum Testamentum*
NRSV	New Revised Standard Version
Oecon.	Xenophon, *Household Management*
Off.	Cicero, *On Duties*
PGM	K. Preisendanz (ed.), *Papyri graecae magicae*
Post. Cain	Philo, *On the Posterity and Exile of Cain*
POxy	B. P. Grenfell and A. S. Hunt (eds.), *Oxyrynchus Papyri*
Praec. Conj.	Plutarch, *Advice to the Bride and Groom*
Protrep.	Clement of Alexandria, *Exhortation to the Greeks*
Quaes. Gen	Philo, *Questions and Solutions on Genesis*
SBLMS	SBL Monograph Series
SBLRBS	SBL Resources for Biblical Study
SNTSMS	Society for New Testament Studies Monograph Series
Sib. Or.	*Sibylline Oracles*
Spec. Leg.	Philo, *On the Special Laws*
T. Benj.	*Testament of Benjamin*
T. Dan	*Testament of Dan*
T. Iss.	*Testament of Issachar*
T. Jud.	*Testament of Judah*
T. Levi	*Testament of Levi*
T. Naph.	*Testament of Naphtali*
T. Reub.	*Testament of Reuben*
T. Sim.	*Testament of Simeon*
Tri. Trac.	*Tripartite Tractate*
UBSGNT	United Bible Societies *Greek New Testament*
Vita Mos.	Philo, *The Life of Moses*
War	Josephus, *The Jewish War*
WBC	Word Biblical Commentary
WUNT	Wissenschaftliche Untersuchungen zum Neuen Testament
ZNW	*Zeitschrift für die neutestamentliche Wissenschaft*

INTRODUCTION

REMEMBERING THE APOSTLE:
GENRE, CHARACTER, AND SOURCES

Although some still argue that Paul was the author of Ephesians (Barth 1974), most scholars agree that the letter is pseudonymous. For an audience accustomed to appropriating all written texts orally—that is, through hearing their contents read and perhaps even explicated by the person who actually conveyed the letter to its recipients—multiple voices in a text were a common experience. Consequently, when scholars speak of Paul as the "implied" or "fictive" author of Ephesians, they do not mean that the writer is making a fraudulent use of Pauline authority. The gap between this letter and Paul's personal correspondence is not hard to detect (Best 1987). Ephesians lacks the personal greetings characteristic of Paul. No associates or fellow Christians are mentioned as co-senders. Those to whom Ephesians speaks do not know the apostle (1:15; 3:2). Yet, as Gentiles who have now been brought into the people of God (2:11-13), they owe a great debt to him. Paul's insight into the mystery of God's saving plan forms the basis of the gospel message (3:1-13). Their familiarity with the apostle has been mediated through writing rather than through his personal presence (3:2-4).

Paul's own letters contain specific details of the relationship between the apostle and those to whom he writes. Figuring out the prior history of the apostle's ministry in a particular church plays a crucial part in understanding those letters. Ephesians has no such clues. Sometimes interpreters supply reasons for a particular theme in Ephesians that have been taken from the context of another of Paul's letters. For example, the assumption that the growing numbers of Gentiles in the church have begun to denigrate the Jewish heritage of Christian faith (a concern of Rom 9–11) is proposed as the reason for writing Ephesians (Martin 1991).

Attempts to construct a setting for Ephesians run up against the literary genre of the work (Meade 1986). The author has adopted ancient rhetorical forms of celebratory and hortatory discourse (see Lincoln 1990, 1995). The first half of the Epistle (1:3–3:21) invites the audience to join in praising and thanking God for the plan of salvation that has united them with Christ. It concludes with a brief doxology (3:20-21). The second half encourages readers to persevere in the social and personal dimensions of their life as a new creation in Christ (4:1–6:20). It concludes in a dramatic peroration (6:10-20). Believers stand armed and ready to vanquish evil powers (6:10-17). They will also assist the imprisoned apostle in continuing his bold witness by remembering him in prayer (6:18-20).

Despite this clear understanding of the genre of the work, Lincoln cannot resist assuming that the rhetorical appeals to the audience built into the genres in question provide information about the Epistle's readers. This methodological difficulty is masked by assuming that such mirror-reading gives access to what literary critics mean by "implied readers." Not so, if the addressees recognize the rhetorical topoi involved. Andrew T. Lincoln comments, "It can be inferred from the implied author's prayers for them (cf. 1.16*b*-19; 3.14-19) and from his appeals which introduce and conclude the parenesis (cf. 4.1-16; 6.10-20) that their main problems are powerlessness, instability and a lack of resolve, and these are related to an insufficient sense of identity" (Lincoln and Wedderburn 1993, 82-83). In fact, these passages tell us nothing about the problems of particular readers, actual or implied. They do establish powerful images of Christian identity. The consolidation of communal identity can be understood as the basic function of celebratory rhetoric. A community that hears praises of its imperial—or, in this case, divine—benefactor, of the peace and well-being that a benefactor's gracious use of power has bestowed on it, that community also comes to know itself in relationship to the benefactor.

The lack of detail even appears in the opening greeting (1:1-2). The phrase "in Ephesus" does not occur in many of the earliest manuscripts. Nor would that locale be appropriate for an audience that does not know the apostle. Paul had worked extensively in Ephesus. He may even have been imprisoned there (1 Cor 15:32). Unlike either Colossians (4:14; 5:6-7) or the Pastorals (1 Tim 1:18-20; 4:1-7), Ephesians never refers to false teachers whose doctrines must be avoided. Therefore the Epistle appears to be addressed to Christian churches in general, not to a particular situation. Some interpreters suggest that the author was concerned with the impact of the pagan religious environment in the Lycus valley and wrote the Epistle as a circular letter to churches in the environs of Laodicea and Hierapolis. Nevertheless, the author does not appear to have any personal knowledge of the addressees. The discourse alternates between the second-person plural "you" and the first-person plural "we." Sometimes "we" designates Jewish Christians associated with the author in contrast to "you" Gentile converts. Sometimes "we" refers to all Christians as a group. Ephesians never uses the common Christian designation "brothers" in addressing the audience. The only use of the term occurs in the conclusion where it is a third-person plural reference.

Ephesians encourages the audience to imitate God (5:1) rather than the apostle, unlike the usual practice in Paul's letters. Even the Pastoral Epistles retain the motif of imitating Paul (2 Tim 1:8; 3:10-14). Since imitation of those who possess virtues is key to ancient parenesis, the absence of the theme in Ephesians highlights the distance between its audience and the apostle (Meade 1986). With the exception of topoi in the Household Code, Ephesians has no significant parallels with the Pastoral Epistles (Lincoln 1990, lvi). Although the author has made extensive use of Colossians, he drops Timothy as co-sender from the opening greeting (1:1 contrast Col 1:1) even though this omission lives on in an odd first-person plural at the end (6:22 contrast Col 4:8). Perhaps this detail is more significant than it appears at first. The author and recipients of Ephesians do not belong to the circle of churches in which Timothy or Paul's other closest associates had been active.

Does Ephesians represent the first introduction these Christians have had to the apostle? Attempts to treat Ephesians as a summary designed to introduce an early collection of Pauline letters (assumed as the referent of 3:3-4) flounder on the genre of the work. Ephesians does not read as an epitome of the apostle's teaching either in its formal rhetorical structure or its content. Further, the passage said to refer to other writings (3:3-4) does not indicate an established canon of Pauline letters. It could refer to the reading of Ephesians as a further explanation of what was said about the mystery in a previous letter. Ephesians may have taken its cue from Col 2:1-6. The apostle's trials are to benefit not only Christians known to him, but others who have never seen him. Ephesians is claiming to express the mystery about which Paul was speaking (so Meade 1986, 150-51).

Verbal comparisons of Ephesians and Colossians are found in the tables that accompany the relevant sections of the commentary. The sum total of such evidence makes a strong case for the view that the author of Ephesians knew and used much of Colossians in his own Epistle. But Ephesians has also recontextualized and changed the order of images and phrases taken from Colossians. Even those sections that are substantially new contain some echoes of Colossians (1:3-14; 2:5-10, 11-18, 19-21; 4:8-16; 5:8-14, 22-33; 6:11-17; so Schnackenburg 1991). Echoes of other Pauline letters are noted in the commentary. Romans is more frequently evident in parallels to Ephesians than any other Pauline letter. Consequently, it does not seem likely that Ephesians relies simply on oral traditions circulating in Pauline churches. Knowledge of some Pauline letters themselves must be presupposed. But one can only make this argument with regard to the author of Ephesians. It is impossible to tell from the Epistle whether or not the recipients were familiar with the passages that we cite as parallels. We will argue that the rhetorical strategies used in the letter presuppose that the audience recognizes what it hears as tradition, not new instruction. Lincoln has suggested using the phrase "actualization of an authoritative tradition" for the reuse of Pauline material in Ephesians (Lincoln 1990, lviii).

David Trobisch's study of letter collections has shed new light on the place of Ephesians in the Pauline corpus. Often the first collection of an author's letters was prepared by the author himself. Trobisch argues that Paul is responsible for creating a collection comprising Romans, 1 and 2 Corinthians, and Galatians. After an author's death other letters would be added at the end of the original group. Finally, someone might prepare a comprehensive collection from all available versions. Trobisch suggests that the first letter to break the principle that orders a collection indicates the point at which such expansion of an existing collection takes place. For the Pauline letters, the ordering principle appears to be length. However, on that criterion, Ephesians should come before Galatians. Therefore, it represents the first Epistle added to the primitive collection produced by the apostle (Trobisch 1994, 50-52). This research tells us nothing about the original addressees or how the Pauline letter canon came to be formed. It only indicates that Ephesians represented the first letter to be added to the originating collection of four major Pauline Epistles.

If the more speculative side of Trobisch's argument holds, namely, that the apostle himself was responsible for Romans through Galatians, then the question of which letters other churches may have possessed looks slightly different. An early collection by the apostle himself may have been designed to be circulated. If Ephesians assumes that its audience has heard actual letters from the apostle, then this group of letters is most likely the group that was circulated. Ephesians may not presume that Colossians was read in the churches to which the apostle writes. Instead, Colossians provided the impetus for Ephesians to formulate Paul's own account of the mystery of salvation.

The basic picture of the apostle that Ephesians leaves with its readers contains few details. He is presented as the great apostle to the Gentiles whose spirit-endowed insight (1:17; 3:2-3) has made the hidden plan of salvation accessible to all. This "mystery" made known through the apostle is also the tradition of the apostles and prophets who are the foundation of the church (2:20-22). Finally, the apostle's imprisonment is "for the sake of you Gentiles" (3:1) and calls for courage to continue boldly proclaiming the gospel (6:19-20). Even these Christians who have no direct connection to the apostle's own churches are assured that the apostle suffers on their behalf. One cannot be sure whether or not the letter's audience knows that Paul has suffered martyrdom. Unlike the letters that Paul wrote from prison earlier, Ephesians never anticipates the possibility of his release. Unlike 2 Tim 4:6-18, Ephesians never hints that his death is near. But the conclusion of Acts indicates that an author and readers who know full well that the apostle has died may celebrate his heroic witness to the gospel without recounting his death.

WHERE EPHESIANS DIFFERS: THEOLOGY, LANGUAGE, AND STYLE

Ephesians was not composed as an epitome of Paul's teaching or as the celebration of an apostle hero. It focuses on God's foreordained plan of salvation, uniting Jew and Gentile in the body of the risen Christ. This theological insight develops a number of themes found in Paul's letters in a new direction. One no longer finds the event of salvation focused on the cross, though the traditional formulae concerning the redemptive effects of Christ's death do appear. Instead of speaking of the power of sin to hold humans in bondage, Ephesians refers to sins in the plural. Bondage is associated with evil powers whose effectiveness is linked to the earthly regions. Consequently, the dominant metaphor for redemption from their influence is exaltation "in the heavenly regions" with the risen Christ (Hultgren 1987, 92-93).

The language of Ephesians also departs markedly from Paul's style. The author constructs extensive, periodic sentences out of dependent clauses introduced by participles and infinitive phrases. In order to provide a readable text, translations break up these long sentences. This commentary is based on the NRSV translation. However, the tables that compare the language of Ephesians with other Pauline letters will provide as literal a rendering as possible in order to indicate similarities of wording. Readers should consult commentaries based on the Greek text for detailed information about the elaborate Greek style in Ephesians. Such commentaries also provide lists of the unusual vocabulary used in Ephesians. Many words are either unique in the New Testament or appear in Ephesians and another New Testament writing, but not elsewhere in the Pauline letters. Some expressions appear to replace Pauline equivalents, for example Ephesians uses "in the heavenly places" (Gk. *en tois ouraniois;* 1:3, 20; 2:6; 3:10; 6:12) where Paul would speak of "in the heavens" (Gk. *en ouranois;* 2 Cor 5:1; Phil 3:20; Col 5:16, 20). Instead of Paul's "Satan," one finds "devil" in Ephesians. The formula used to introduce citations from scripture "therefore it says" (Gk. *dio legei*) is also not found in Pauline letters and the expression "good works" in the plural (2:10) does not appear there, though it does occur in the Pastorals (see Schnackenburg 1991, 25-27).

Other features of Pauline letter form are missing, such as expressions of confidence, the formal opening to the body of a letter with a request or disclosure formula. The apostle typically uses a *charis* (translated "thanks") formula as a contrast to a previously described negative situation (for example 2 Cor 2:12-15; Belleville 1991). Ephesians does not use such contrastive formulae. Instead, *charis* (translated "grace") appears as the foundation of salvation and appears in expressions where one would expect "faith" if Paul had composed the letter (for example, "by grace you have been saved through faith," 2:8). Or one would anticipate a discussion of righteousness in connection with the salvation of the Gentiles in 2:8-10. Instead, Ephesians refers to grace as the gift of God in opposition to works. The term "works" also appears without Paul's normal qualifier "of the Law." In verse 10, the non-Pauline plural "good works" appears to refer to the moral conduct of those who are in Christ. The term "law" only appears in 2:15, where the "law with its commandments and ordinances" has been canceled by the cross. There is no more distinction between Jew and Gentile. The whole complex of linguistic formulae that the apostle created to describe the inclusion of Gentiles in the promise of salvation has vanished with hardly a trace (Schnackenburg 1991, 26-27; Lincoln and Wedderburn 1993).

This shift may be grounded in rhetoric as well as theology. Marc Schoeni's study of the "how much the more" formulae in Romans 5 discovered an important semantic distinction between using the topic "justification" and using "reconciliation." The language of justification is structured in such a way that it discriminates and divides. It acknowledges the singular differences between Jew and

Gentile. Reconciliation "sublates and unites." By incorporating the differentiated singularities into a greater whole, reconciliation denies their significance (Schoeni 1993, 181). Though Paul works with both reconciliation and justification, Ephesians has taken the reconciliation imagery of Rom 5:1-11 to be the Pauline understanding of salvation. Consequently, distinctions in Paul's terminology will be overridden by unity.

Several linguistic shifts are associated with the term "mystery." Ephesians often uses expressions that have their closest parallels in the Essene writings from Qumran where we find the "mystery" of the divine plan of salvation hidden in the prophets until the end time. Paul also uses "mystery" for God's preordained eschatological plan of salvation. "Mystery" designates different aspects of the overall plan of salvation: (a) 1 Cor 2:1, 7, the crucifixion; (b) 1 Cor 15:51, the end-time transformation of the righteous into resurrected bodies, and (c) Rom 11:25, the present hardening of Israel as a condition for salvation of the Gentiles to be followed by salvation for "all Israel." In 1 Cor 4:1, Paul refers to the apostles, specifically himself and Apollos, as "stewards of God's mysteries," and uses the term in a general way for revealed knowledge in 1 Cor 13:2 (also 14:2, ironically?). Its use for the salvation of the Gentiles as hidden in the prophets until the present at Rom 16:25-27 may be an addition to the letter, but it maintains the overtones of apocalyptic revelation characteristic of Paul's usage.

When Paul applies the term "mystery" to his gospel in Rom 11:25, he is not only thinking of God's plan to summon all humanity to salvation but he is also thinking of the story of Israel. God's promises to the covenant people, and their apparent inability to recognize Christ as the fulfillment of the Law issue in Paul's conviction that God must still bring salvation to Israel. For Ephesians, only the first side of Paul's thought remains: God intends to bring all to salvation in Christ (3:8-9). This mystery is grounded in the will of God from the beginning (1:9) and has been made known through the preaching of the apostle (6:19). It is also embodied in his writing (3:3-4). These examples are easily viewed as developments of Paul's own usage. After the apostle's death it would be natural to consider the written expression of his gospel as the way in which the mystery becomes known to others. However, a more significant shift becomes evident when Ephesians is compared with the immediate source for these expressions, Colossians (1:27; 2:2; 4:3). In every one of the Colossians examples the shorthand that clarifies the term "mystery" is "Christ." For Colossians, the mystery is the fact that salvation comes to all people through faith in Christ.

Ephesians shifts the playing field. The focus of the mystery is not the cosmic Christ of Colossians but the Body of Christ, the church. The problem is not how Gentiles can participate in God's salvation while remaining free from the Law. Instead, Ephesians conceives the problem as one of unity. The series of "with . . ." or "co-" terms in Eph 3:6 makes this point about the church, the Gentiles are "heirs with," "body with" and "sharers of the promise in Christ through the gospel" (AT). This perspective makes it quite natural for Ephesians to speak of the union of Christ, the head, with his Body, the church, as a "mystery" (Eph 5:32).

This use of "Body of Christ" goes beyond Paul's own use of the expression. Paul employed a common image from the political philosophy of his day to appeal for order and harmony in the Corinthian church. Christians should understand that the Spirit has provided diverse gifts within the community so that the whole body can function together. Strife over gifts among Christians is as absurd as parts of the body claiming that they do not belong because they are not some other part (1 Cor 12:12-31). The image is repeated in the same sense in Rom 12:3-8. He can also extend the metaphor of Christians as members of the "Body of Christ" to argue for appropriate separation from the two forms of immorality that Jews commonly associated with paganism—sexual immorality (1 Cor 6:15) and idolatrous cultic practices (1 Cor 10:17). Thus for the apostle the expression "Body of Christ" involves a metaphor for how to order the concrete details of everyday Christian life. Like the term "church" in Paul's letters, the term "Body of Christ" designates local communities of Christians (Yorke 1991).

Ephesians does not address a local community. Its vision of the church is set in the largest possible framework, the cosmic body of all the faithful united with its head, the risen Christ (1:22-23; 2:6).

When the image of church as "Body of Christ" comes into the ethical exhortation, the picture is one of a "new human being" growing into the Body of Christ that serves under its head (4:13-16). Paul's reference to concrete gifts of ministry in the body are incorporated into this larger vision of the church as the agent through whom its growth takes place (4:11-12). The development toward a more cosmic image of "Body of Christ" is anticipated in the hymnic tradition. Colossians 1:15-20 depicts Christ first as divine wisdom active in creation, then as redeemer. Christ, the redeemer, is head of the body that is the church by virtue of being "firstborn from the dead" (Col 1:18). Colossians 1:19 introduces another term that will figure in the cosmic vision of church found in Ephesians, "fullness." For Colossians, "fullness" refers to divinity dwelling in Christ. For Ephesians, it will refer to the way in which Christ dwells in the cosmic Body, the church (1:23; 3:19; 4:13).

Other metaphors used for the church are drawn into this picture of the church as "Body of Christ." It can be described as a building or temple being built up into Christ (2:20-21). Christians are members of God's household as children of God, not as strangers or resident aliens (2:19). Because the "Body of Christ" is depicted as a heavenly reality, some of the attributes that describe the church follow as natural consequences. The church must be a unity (2:14-16; 4:1-3, 10-13), holy (1:3-8; 4:17-22; 5:3-5, 25-27), universal (2:16; 3:1-6). It cannot be considered part of this world as though it were a socio-political institution (5:18-20; Yorke 1991, 101-3). If it were, the church would be subject to the powers and authorities that govern the lower regions. Because the body of Christ is the preordained vehicle by which God has chosen to unite all things with Godself and to subjugate the lower powers (3:10), the church has always belonged to the divine plan of salvation. The doxology of 3:21 insists that God is praised "in the church and in Christ Jesus."

Those who consider such a vision of the church as a dangerous precedent should attend to the metaphors used. None of them attach the reality of the cosmic Body of Christ to a particular group of human authorities. No single community could embody the church. Rudolf Schnackenburg remarks, "For the author all the congregations which lie within his field of vision do not yet, even taken together, constitute 'the ecclesia.' This is rather an entity which has precedence over all, in which they participate and in accordance with which they should orient their lives" (Schnackenburg 1991, 295). Similarly the "mystery" of the church united to Christ as bride thus transforms a common Jewish metaphor for Israel as the "bride of Yahweh" (Hos 1–3; Ezek 16; Jer 2:2; Isa 65:5) by highlighting the realism of the unity between Christ and the church. Christ's self-offering on the cross is the foundation of her holiness (Eph 5:2, 25). Christ's loving concern for the welfare of the church extends to the realities of Christian life in this world. It is not merely a reference to the heavenly unity of the saints with their head (2:5-6). If Ephesians can use this concern to describe the conduct of husbands toward their wives in marriage, then it should also be reflected in the ways that Christian leaders go about their various ministries.

The references to such ministries in Ephesians also create some difficulties. When Paul refers to himself as apostle (1:1) or servant of the gospel chosen by God to make God's salvation known to the Gentiles (3:7-9), we are on familiar ground. The self-deprecating comment, "although I am the very least of all the saints, this grace was given to me" (3:8) sounds close to Paul's own account of his apostleship (1 Cor 15:8-10). But Ephesians appears to have slipped out of the apostolic perspective in Eph 3:5. The mystery unknown to previous generations has now been revealed to God's "holy apostles and prophets by the Spirit." Since "prophets" follows the reference to apostles, the speaker does not appear to mean the Old Testament prophets. The author appears to be looking back on a revelation transmitted by Christian apostles and prophets. When Paul refers to Christian prophets, they are not associated with the apostolic witness to the gospel. Their function involves speaking, prayer, and exhortation within the local assembly (1 Cor 11:2-16; 14:29, 32, 37). When he refers to other apostles positively, Paul highlights the unity of his message with theirs (see 1 Cor 15:11).

Ephesians 2:20 puts "apostles and prophets" in the past. They are the foundation of the building, the church, which is growing into Christ. By contrast, Paul describes himself as the master builder who builds on the foundation, Jesus Christ (1 Cor 3:10-14). The parenetic section of the letter treats the term "apostles" as first in a list of gifts to the church: apostles, prophets, evangelists, pastors and teachers (4:11). They are to equip Christians for service in building up the body of Christ until all attain maturity, the fullness of Christ (4:12-13). Once again the relationship between such persons and local church communities remains undefined. Only the last two, pastors and teachers, clearly designate resident leaders of the local church. The terms may not describe any particular church order. Ephesians merely wishes to indicate in a general way that God has charged certain persons with nurturing the church by aiding others to grow in unity and knowledge of God. This concern for harmony, internal unity, and growth might represent the concerns of a church facing the death of the apostolic generation.

The cosmic picture of the church already united with the risen Christ shifts attention away from the end-time coming of the Lord (as in 1 Thess 4:13–5:11). For Paul, all things are not yet subjected to Christ. When they are, when every authority and power is destroyed, then Christ will bring all under God's rule (1 Cor 15:24-28). Ephesians refers to the subjection of all authorities and powers as a present reality. The risen and exalted Christ is far above all powers whether in this age or the age to come (Eph 1:19-23). Similarly, believers have been freed from the powers of darkness and raised up with Christ in the heavens. This exaltation also demonstrates God's extraordinary graciousness toward the faithful in the coming ages (Eph 2:5-7). Elements of future eschatology remain part of the author's conceptual world, but they do not serve as criteria to determine one's present position in the world. Nor is a culminating event in God's saving plan anticipated in the near future. Ephesians never uses the term "mystery" to designate a future act of redemption. The mystery of bringing all things together in Christ may not be completed, but it has already become a reality in the church (1:10).

This eschatological shift is evident in another formal difference between Ephesians and other Pauline letters. The apostle typically concludes major sections with references to elements of future judgment or salvation (for example Rom 11:31-36; 1 Cor 1:9-10;

15:54-58; Phil 1:10-11; 3:20–4:1; 1 Thess 1:9-10; 2:19-20; 3:11-13). Such references carry a hortatory message to the audience, take care to persevere so that God may "strengthen your hearts in holiness that you may be blameless before our God and Father at the coming of our Lord Jesus with all his saints" (1 Thess 3:13). Ephesians retains the liturgical character of Pauline transitions by using formulaic expressions (as in 1:20-23) or doxologies (as in 3:20-21). It uses "saints" as its designation for believers (e.g., 1:1, 15; 2:19; 3:18; 5:3; 6:18). Concerns that the church be "holy and blameless" are reflected in the opening prayer (1:4) and the parenesis (4:24; 5:27) but never appear with the reference to the Lord coming in judgment. The conclusion to the whole letter (6:10-20) takes up the motif of divine armor, which occurs as part of the eschatological conclusion to 1 Thessalonians (1 Thess 5:8). Even here, where one would expect standing fast to be accompanied by an explicit indication that these are the "last days" there is no reference to a judgment day. All that remains are the linguistic tags "withstand on that evil day" (6:13) and "keep alert" (6:18). Ephesians never speaks of Christ coming in judgment. Its ecclesiology short-circuits such language, since the church already exists in the unity of the saints with their exalted head.

Searching for a Context: Author and Occasion

Scholars have mined various features of the letter to construct a background for its author or audience. Since the destination "Ephesus" was not original, those theories built on archaeological and religious descriptions of ancient Ephesus and its Artemis cult have no foundation in the text. Some advocates of an Ephesus argument claim that the pluralism of religious cults and magic practices evident there are representative of the environment of cities in Asia Minor. Since the emphasis on Christ's exaltation above the powers of the cosmos and the identification of believers with their exalted head forms the center of Ephesians, this imagery might be read as a response to pagan religion. The Artemis cult in Ephesus demonstrates the superiority of the goddess to all forces; she is queen of the cosmos, as the signs of the zodiac around her neck and the magic letters on her scepter demonstrate. Associated with her, one finds Hecate, goddess of the underworld (Arnold 1989). Similar zodiac imagery is connected with other goddess figures like Diana and Isis. Funerary reliefs at Philippi depict the deified male or female child being conducted into heavenly places (Abrahamsen 1995). Other authors compare the "seated in the heavenly places" of Ephesians with the heavenly ascent of Mithraism (Cargal 1994). These parallels say little about the details of Ephesians, but they suggest religious images and prior convictions that its audience would bring with them to the letter.

Other interpreters follow the lead of classic commentaries (especially Schlier 1957) and look to ancient Gnostic mythologies. The separation between the heavenly regions in which those with knowledge of God are linked with the redeemer and the lower world of darkness governed by hostile forces forms a central element in their speculation. The second and third century CE Gnostic texts provide suggestive parallels to some of the images in Ephesians. Gnostic writers claim Ephesians as evidence that the apostle taught a Gnostic doctrine of the soul fallen from heaven and trapped by hostile powers. Once awakened and enlighted by the heavenly revealer from heaven, the soul is superior to the powers. However, peculiarly Gnostic terminology or theologoumena do not appear in Ephesians, so emerging Gnostic sectarianism does not provide a hermeneutical framework for reading the Epistle.

Some interpreters have tried to combine all of these motifs. A Gnostic dualism between the heavenly and earthly regions is said to cause the turn toward astrology and magic in order to gain security in a dangerous, hostile universe (Martin 1991). Or they assume that since Ephesians speaks of access to God through the knowledge that comes in Christ, it must be opposed to visionaries who claim to have ascended into heaven and to have been seated in God's presence (Gouldner 1994). Such visionary practices linked to Jewish speculation about heavenly realities have been more easily linked to the false teaching rejected in Col 2:8–3:4 (Dunn 1995). Though Ephesians adopts the concluding image of believers seeking what belongs to the risen Christ (Col 3:1-4), none of the polemic details of the Colossians text are found in Ephesians. Further, as we have seen above, Ephesians erases the eschatological reservation found in earlier Pauline letters. Colossians limits the believers' identification with the exalted Christ to the future coming of Christ. For Ephesians, the saints are already one with their Lord. Once again, Ephesians shows no evidence of engaging a particular religious situation.

Since Ephesians highlights the incorporation of Gentiles with Israel in the new creation that God had planned from the beginning (2:11-18; 3:6), a natural context would appear to have been relationships between Jewish and Gentile Christians. Some interpreters lift the problematic of Gentile conversion from Pauline Epistles to explain the need for their ethical instruction in Ephesians. But though the center of the apostle's gospel did require that both Jew and Gentile be made righteous on the same basis, through faith (Gal 2:15-21), Ephesians never deals with those concrete details of the Law that distinguish Jew and Gentile. Ephesians can refer to "circumcision" and "uncircumcision" as markers of the two communities (2:11) without any indication that the distinction created a problem for relationships between Jewish and Gentile Christians in their unity. Contrast Colossians where circumcision is spiritualized (2:11), and Jewish sabbaths, holy days, and food laws are rejected (2:16-17). Ephesians 2:15 refers without difficulty to the "law with its commandments and ordinances" abolished by the cross. Consequently, many scholars agree that the churches to which Ephesians is written cannot include an active, Jewish Christian group.

If the community envisaged by the letter consists solely of Gentiles being encouraged to remember themselves as brought into a common inheritance with Jewish believers, does the reminder provide any hints about the setting of the letter? Many of our best parallels to its religious concepts can be found among the Essene texts from Qumran. Such comparisons along with the exegetical forms used by the author suggest a person with a background in first-century CE Jewish sectarianism. At the same time, the ornate Greek rhetorical style suggests a Jew with a hellenistic education. This combination is similar to that of Paul himself. In Paul's case, the sectarian piety through which he assimilated Judaism was Pharisaism. In this case, it was some form of sectarian piety closer to that of the Essenes. The author of Ephesians not only looks to the apostle Paul as the recipient of special understanding of God's plan, he is also a student of Paul's letters. Given the Essene interest in texts, including preserving and continuing an exegetical tradition linked to its founder, one might infer that such a person had made an effort to obtain copies of Paul's letters.

Other interpreters suggest that Ephesians attempts to ward off a crisis similar to that addressed by Paul in Rom 11:17-36. Its repeated use of "with . . ." formulae as well as the priority given "us" into which "you," Gentiles, have been incorporated indicates a desire to hang on to the Jewish roots of Christianity (Meade 1986, 146). But Ephesians has surrendered the careful distinction between the church and Israel so important to Paul. Its exhortations have nothing to do with Judaism. Rather, the Gentile audience must remain committed to the new Christian way of life, to worship, to mutual love and assistance among believers, and to the moral reform that marks them as "children of God."

On the one hand, it seems more accurate to think of the early Christian movement as an "internal migration" of a sectarian group within Judaism than as a "new religion" (so Georgi 1995, who does not deal with Ephesians). On the other, Ephesians clearly perceives the Jew and Gentile believers who constitute the body of the risen Christ as a "new creation," not merely the righteous remnant of Israel with some Gentiles thrown in. For its readers, the existence of any actual relationships with the Jewish communities of Asia Minor remains in doubt.

Ephesians presumes that preaching the gospel involves persuading others to turn away from paganism as cultic practice and from moral laxity in one's conduct to become part of the Christian community. But does this orientation reflect an attitude that the Gentile Christian mission assimilated from the hellenistic synagogue? Martin Goodman has recently assembled considerable evidence against the view that either Jews or pagans thought that it would be preferable if all humans worshiped the same God (Goodman 1994). Scholars find the social boundaries of those Gentile

sympathizers often referred to as "god-fearers" increasingly difficult to fix clearly. Clearly some outsiders found their way into
Judaism as proselytes (see Tob 1:8; Josephus *C. Apion* ii §210).
When women of the Herodian family married, they required that
their husbands be converted to Judaism (Josephus *Ant.* xx §139,
145; Goodman 1994, 63-65). In some areas, though by no means
everywhere, one finds Jewish communities with a range of Gentile
sympathizers or benefactors. Why would outsiders act as benefactors to the Jewish community? They must have been encouraged
that such acts would have a reward (cf. Rom 2:12-16). Persons
within the Jewish community may have encouraged such benefactors whose assistance they required in order to maintain the political
independence of their community (Goodman 1994, 87-88).

Would such Gentiles have been drawn to the early Christian
movement as Acts suggests (see Acts 16:11-14; 17:1-5)? Some
synagogue benefactors clearly retained their pagan ties and even
priesthoods within pagan cult associations (Trebilco 1991, 58-59).
If that was a normal pattern of benefaction, then the language of
Ephesians that highlights the radical break of conversion might be
directed toward those who thought that they could retain earlier
associations while belonging to the Christian group (as in 1 Cor
10:1-22, for example). What else these Gentiles from Asia Minor
might have known about Jews can only be suggested by supple-
menting the few hints in the letter with general evidence for the
region. Ephesians itself assumes that readers are familiar with
"circumcision" as the decisive criterion for belonging to Israel, with
Jewish monotheism and its critique of pagan gods, with Scripture,
and in a general way with Jews as separated from non-Jews by
"commandments and ordinances." None of these observations go
beyond what ordinary Gentiles might know about Jews. Indeed,
Ephesians does not refer to the other common items of information,
Sabbath observance and food laws, even though they appear in
Colossians. This omission may indicate that Jewish or Jewish
Christian practice was not an issue.

Early Christian churches appear in those cities of Asia Minor that
also had Jewish communities. Louis Feldman suggests that the lack
of Pharisaic influence in the inland cities of Asia Minor indicates

that Judaism there was less bound to the land of Israel. Jewish inscriptions lack the pious Jewish sentiments of longing for the Temple or artistic representations of the ark or the menorah so common elsewhere. Sardis appears to have been the exception to the rule of a lower degree of Jewish identity in inland Asia Minor. Its large, wealthy, and properous community evoked sharp anti-Jewish polemic from Melito, Bishop of Sardis in the second century. Even in the fourth century, the remodeled Jewish synagogue was a larger and more impressive building than the Christian church (Feldman 1993, 73). If the relative strength and social prestige of the two communities were as Feldman suggests, such that the Jewish community far outweighed that of the Christian offshoot, then the emphasis on Jewish origins evident in Ephesians might serve to intensify communal identity among the Christian minority.

After all, Ephesians makes the extraordinary claim that God's plan for humanity is represented by this community. Some have even compared that language to claims for the peace created by the Roman Empire (Mussner 1982). Though there is no clear evidence that Ephesians is concerned with imperial ideology, the suggestion points to the spiritual importance of its message. The case for creating unity through imperial expansion was evident in the architecture of the great cities of Asia Minor. The Jewish community in many Asia Minor cities owed Roman power an important debt; appeals to Roman authorities secured Jewish rights to sabbath observance, protection of money collected for the Jerusalem Temple and the like. Ephesians envisages a different basis for human unity, a religious one. As far as one can tell, this realization was unique to the Christian mission. Not even the Romans thought that all the citizens of their empire would worship Roman gods. Jews never undertook a policy of proselytism to bring pagans to the worship of God. Ephesians has set Paul's own concern for a mission that would reach the ends of the Roman Empire (Rom 15:18-23) in a global perspective. God planned to unite all things in Christ even before creation.

COMMENTARY

GREETING (1:1-2)

Ancient letters begin with a greeting that identifies the sender and recipients. Pauline letters expand the traditional formula with expressions of Christian faith or references to the divine origin of Paul's apostolic authority (1 Cor 1:1-3; Col 1:1-2). Some ancient manuscripts lack the words "in Ephesus." Without a concrete place reference, the greeting is grammatically awkward, since the designation "to the saints" is followed by the words "who are and faithful." The translation in the NRSV note, "to the saints who are also faithful," treats the "and" (Gk. *kai*) as "also" rather than as a conjunction. (On the grammatical problems of this translation see Lincoln 1990, 2.) Though there are no ancient examples, some commentators suggest that Ephesians was originally a circular letter into which the name of a particular church could be inserted. Since Ephesians reformulates sections from Colossians, one would expect the addressees to be designated "to the saints in Ephesus" (cf. Col 1:2). The "grace and peace" formula (v. 2) adds "and the Lord Jesus Christ" (see Rom 1:7) to Col 1:2. Conflation of Col 1:1-2 with Rom 1:7 may explain the dangling "who are" since Rom 1:7 has "to all those *who are* in Rome" (the NRSV changes the sentence structure).

◊ ◊ ◊ ◊

1-2: Assuming that the author was a disciple of Paul who used Colossians and other Pauline letters to compose a letter of instruction explains the lack of precision about the addressees. Ephesians indicates that Paul was unknown to its audience (so 1:15; 3:2), but such personal distance would not be true of Ephesus, where the apostle spent considerable time (Acts 19:1-22) and from which he wrote to the Corinthians. Ephesus was probably the locus of the "mortal threat" mentioned in 2 Cor 1:8-11 (also 1 Cor 15:32), possibly the imprisonment of Phil 1 and 2. The ties between Paul and Ephesus explain how an ancient scribe attached "in Ephesus" to this text. The mention of Tychicus as the letter carrier in Eph 6:21 combined with the assertion that he was sent to Ephesus in 2 Tim 4:12 could also generate the address.

Expressions found in the greeting are central to the letter's depiction of the author and his audience. Surprisingly, the author never again speaks of himself as "apostle." Instead, the word "apostle" appears in lists of those whose past activities provide the foundation for the church (2:20; 3:5; 4:11). The letter's "Paul" speaks of himself as the imprisoned ambassador for a gospel that revealed God's saving plan for the Gentiles (3:1-13; 4:1; 6:19-20). The reference to the "will of God" introduces a theme that is echoed in the rest of the letter. The "will of God" lies behind the plan that the Gentiles would be included in salvation (1:5, 9, 11). The phrase appears in the hortatory material to highlight the orientation of Christian life (5:17; 6:6).

Of the two terms used to describe the addressees, "faithful" and "saints" ("holy ones"), the former never returns except in reference to Tychicus (6:21, from Col 4:7) but "saints" echoes throughout the letter. It is a standard designation for members of the Christian community (1:15, 18; 2:19; 3:8, 18; 4:12; 5:3; 6:18), but it also designates the moral purity to which Christians are called (1:4; 5:3, 27). A common self-designation among early Christians (see Rom 1:7; 1 Cor 1:2; 2 Cor 1:1; Acts 9:13), the expression was taken from Old Testament references to Israel as a people set apart for the Lord (Lev 11:44; 19:2; 20:26). Its primary emphasis in the Old Testament is not moral perfection but the dedication of persons, places, or objects to the service of God (Exod 28:2; Pss 2:6; 24:3). These cultic connotations emerge in Ephesians when Christians are described as "a holy temple" (Eph 2:21).

Paul regularly replaced the secular epistolary "greeting" with "grace and peace" (see Rom 1:7; Phil 1:2; Gal 1:3; 1 Cor 1:3). God is "father" both of the "Lord Jesus Christ" (Eph 1:3; see 2 Cor 1:3; Rom 15:6) and of believers, who are God's adopted children in

Christ (Eph 1:5; see Gal 4:4-7; Rom 8:14-17). Their access to God as Father is possible through the Spirit (Eph 2:18; see Gal 4:6; Rom 8:16, 27). God as our common "Father" is the focus of both prayer (Eph 3:14; 5:20) and the unity of the church that God's activity has brought into being (Eph 4:6). However, there is a change in how Ephesians uses the language of God as "Father." Ephesians does not correlate it with references to either Jesus as "son" ("Son of God" only appears in 4:13) or believers as "sons." Instead, Christians attain their special relationship to God because they belong to the exalted, heavenly Christ who is head of the Body, a new creation of the perfect human. References to God as "Father" occur either in set formulae of blessing, prayer, or confession (1:2, 3, 17; 4:5; 6:23) or in references to prayer (2:18; 3:14; 5:20).

Another shift in imagery attaches to the theological use of the terms "grace" and "peace." "Grace" appears as a well-understood agent of salvation (2:5, 8); as an attribute of God that merits human praise (1:6-7; 2:7); as God's gift to Paul for the ministry he carries out (3:2-8); or as a gift to individual believers (4:7). "Peace" appears in a central image for the "mystery" of God's saving activity: the reconciliation of Jew and Gentile in one new human being (Eph 2:15-17). That image reshapes the exhortation to peace within the community (Eph 4:3).

Whether directed to an individual, a particular community, or—as appears to have been the case with Ephesians—to several churches, the Pauline letter was always a public event. Colossians 4:16 speaks of the reading and exchange of letters between churches in neighboring cities. The power of a whole letter, read out to an expectant community, is an important part of the event of communication. Ephesians uses the conventional greeting formulae to ready the audience for the reading that follows. Hearing the letter will remind them of how God and the Lord Jesus Christ have reshaped their lives. The ornate rhetorical style sweeps the audience up into the author's vision of membership in a cosmic church united with its exalted head.

EULOGY ON SALVATION (1:3-14)

Greek letters usually followed the greeting with a brief thanks-giving or wish for the health of recipients. Pauline letters have transformed that feature into a longer thanksgiving for their faith, which also telegraphs themes found in the body of the letter (see Rom 1:8-9, 10-15; Phil 1:3-11; Col 1:3-8). In 2 Cor 1:3-11 the opening takes the form of a Blessing (2 Cor 1:3*a*). Ephesians employs both the Blessing (1:3-14) and the Thanksgiving prayer report (1:15-23). Each consists of a single sentence, elaborately crafted from a sequence of subordinate participial and prepositional clauses. English translations break up these sentences into shorter sentences.

Unlike the undisputed Pauline letters, Ephesians does not refer in this section to the situation of its audience. Instead, the Blessing period evokes the liturgical origin of the blessing formula as found in the Psalms (LXX 66:20; 68:35). The liturgical sense of blessing (Gk. *eulogein*) God for deeds of salvation has been combined with the rhetorical understanding of "eulogy" as eloquence or fine speaking in praise of someone. Thus Ephesians telegraphs its intention to the audience. We are about to hear a fine speech in praise of "God [the] Father of our Lord Jesus Christ." True to the rhetorical conventions of such speech, Ephesians indicates that such praise is the appropriate response to benefits conferred. In the secular sphere, speech in praise of a benefactor might elicit future benefactions by cementing the relationship between a powerful individual and those who participate in his praise.

Ephesians takes up this tradition by repeatedly underlining the fact that the blessings that its audience has received come from a beneficent God who consistently intended to confer salvation. The passage is punctuated by references to election and divine will (vv. 4, 5, 9, 11). Another set of phrases refer to the praise that the recipients of salvation owe their divine benefactor (vv. 6, 12, 14). The conclusion treats the present experience of salvation as the guarantee of a future inheritance and ongoing praise of God's glory. Ephesians weaves the function of Christ as heavenly mediator into the praise of God as benefactor. A series of clauses beginning with "in whom" spell out the Christian promise of salvation (vv. 7-10, 11-12, 13-14). The NRSV has created sentences that focus our attention on the benefits of salvation received in Christ: God blessed us in Christ (vv. 3-4) and destined us for adoption in Christ (vv. 5-6); redemption is through the blood of Christ (vv. 7-8*a*); knowledge of God's will unites all things in Christ (vv. 8*b*-10); we are destined to praise God in Christ (vv. 11-12), and Gentiles [= "you"] are included in this inheritance through preaching the gospel (vv. 13-14). Verses 9-10 have a central place in the theological understanding of Ephesians. The exaltation of Christ in the heavens provides the foundation for bringing the entire creation into unity under Christ as head. Appropriately, the final words of verse 14 pick up the intent of the whole section, "to the praise of his [= God's] glory."

◊ ◊ ◊ ◊

The biblical tradition insists that praise is the appropriate human response to God's acts of salvation (Pss 96:1-4; 118:1). Without the appearance of Jesus, God's full plan for salvation would have remained hidden (vv. 9-10). The expression "every spiritual blessing" highlights the completeness of divine salvation. Unlike human benefactors, God has not conferred a partial blessing. Jewish roots for this expression lie in the blessing of Joseph by Jacob (Gen 49:25) and in the liturgical language of the Essenes, "May [my Lord] bless you [from his holy residence]. . . . May he bestow upon you all the blessings [. . .] in the congregation of the holy ones," (1QSb 1:3-5). The reference to "the holy ones" assimilates the Essene congregation to the angels who are in the heavens with God.

Ephesians has modified this Jewish form by substituting the exalted Christ for the angelic hosts and using a peculiar plural form, "the heavenlies" (NRSV: "the heavenly places"), to refer to heaven. That expression only appears in Ephesians where it is used both for God's dwelling (1:3, 20; 2:6) and for a sphere in which hostile powers are active (3:10; 6:12). Descriptions of the universe in the first century CE assumed that the earth was in the center of a cosmos that stretched out to the sphere of the stars. The moon, sun, and planets (through Saturn) circled the earth. The region from the earth to the moon was one in which decay and death occurred. Earthy, heavy, watery, and dark substances tended toward the earth. Fire and air tended toward the heavens. In order to reach the realm of the divine, the soul would have had to ascend through all of these heavenly regions. Spiritual beings, sometimes depicted as demonic, could be associated with the planetary spheres and their power to dictate the fate of humans and nations.

This picture of the cosmos was replicated in Jewish apocalypses that described the ascent of a seer to a vision of the divine throne. By the first century CE most apocalypses assumed that the journey would require passing through multiple heavens (Himmelfarb 1993, 32; see *T. Levi* 2–3; 8; *2 Enoch* 3–21; *Apoc. Mos.* 35:2; 2 Cor 12:1-3). Ordinarily the fear or awe felt by the visionary is mitigated by the protection of his angelic guide. Ephesians does not develop the details of multiple heavenly regions.

The explanation in verse 4 picks up the agency of Christ as the mediator of salvation and expands the description of God's plan of salvation in a temporal direction. God's plan to redeem humanity preexists the foundation of the world. The image of God's election of the righteous and condemnation of the wicked prior to creation appears in Essene texts (CD 2:7; 1QS 1:10-11). According to these texts God ordained the course of all the cosmic powers as well as those of humankind in his act of creation (1QH 9[= 1]:10-20; 1QS 3:15-17). Ephesians agrees with the Essene view that the elect follow the paths of holiness that God established for his creatures. The formulation in verse 4 does not imply the preexistence of the individual souls of the righteous. Nor does Ephesians spell out the connection between the Christ in whom the righteous are elect and God's creative activity. Its emphasis is on the experience of salvation. Those who come to believe in Christ find themselves participating in God's eternal plan.

The phrase "in love" at the conclusion of verse 4 appears so awkward that some have treated it as the motive for the divine "destined" (that is, "predestined") in verse 5. However, it matches the phrase, "in the Beloved," which concludes verse 6. Therefore, the expression appears to be a stylistic marker. It may be intended to refer to divine election in Christ rather than to human behavior.

Verses 5-6 develop the previous reference to divine election in Christ by introducing the Pauline motif of adoption (Gal 4:4-7; Rom 8:15-23). A striking difference between the use of predestination language in Ephesians and similar expressions found at Qumran is the lack of any reference to the wicked. Ephesians knows such language, as later references to "those who are disobedient" indicate (2:2-3; 5:6). But in keeping with the author's vision of unity, God's gracious election could not be expressed as the sharp division of humankind into a righteous remnant, the holy elect, over against a majority who will never experience God's grace. Predestination also has this positive tenor in Paul's usage (see Rom 8:29-30; 1 Cor 2:7).

The description of election in Ephesians is consistently theocentric. God calls a people "for himself." Consequently, the Greek of verse 5a follows "adoption through Christ" with the prepositional phrase "in him" (Gk. *eis auton*), which refers to God rather than to the Son. This focus diverges from the Pauline formula in Rom 8:29, which treats the calling of the elect as necessary to provide brothers and sisters for Christ the firstborn. Verse 6 spells out the reason for the existence of the elect community: worship and praise of the one whose gracious benefits they have received through the Beloved [= Jesus Christ].

Traditional Christian formulae underlie the description in verses 7-8 of how believers receive grace through Christ: his death brings forgiveness of sins. Ephesians 1:7 adds "through his blood" and the conclusion "according to the riches of his [= God's] grace" to a formula from Col 1:14. The term "redemption" (also see Rom 3:24) can be used for freeing a slave (LXX Dan 4:34; Exod 21:8). God obtained Israel as a people for himself by liberating them from Egypt (Exod 15:16; Ps 74:2) or from captivity (Isa 51:11). Since it also came to refer to God's end-time action on Israel's behalf (Isa 59:29; Ps 130:7-8), early Christian usage points to Christ's death as effecting this salvation. The formula quoted in Rom 3:24-26 indicates that Christ's death was understood as the expiation for sin that makes redemption—God's free gift to believers—a reality.

The present tense of the verb "we have" (v. 7) suggests that Christ continues to be the source of deliverance from sin for believers.

Verse 8 specifies the expression of God's graciousness as "wisdom and insight" bestowed on believers. In the Old Testament, insight and wisdom are characteristic of the pious who attend to God's revelation by living according to the Law (Prov 1:2-7; 2:2-10; Ps 37:30-31). The Dead Sea Scrolls speak of wisdom or understanding of God's way as a special gift to the teacher(s) of the sect (1QH 5[= 13]:7-9; 6[= 14]:8-9, 25-27). This revelation separates the sectaries from the rest of humanity who lack wisdom and understanding (1QS 11:5-6). Thus, understanding forms part of the imagery of election. Characteristic of its modification of such metaphors, Ephesians bypasses the dualistic framework in the Qumran texts.

The Essene examples include other virtues along with understanding: deeds of truth instead of sin, justice, loving what God loves, hatred of evil, love of God, wholehearted devotion to the quest for wisdom. The ethical section of Ephesians (4:1–6:20) takes up the concrete expression of such understanding in Christian life. Verse 9 with its reference to "mystery," continues to parallel the language of election found in the Essene writings. The Aramaic equivalent to "mystery," *raz* (Dan 2:18), appears in Essene interpretation of prophetic texts to refer to the secret plan of God's salvation that has been revealed to the sectaries (1QpHab 7:1-4, 13-14; 8:1-3). Paul uses "mystery" in this sense to refer to God's plan for the salvation of humanity in Christ. It has a future reference, that Jews who reject Christ will be included in salvation (Rom 11:25-32). Paul designates the presence of salvation unknown to the rulers of the cosmos when they crucified the Lord of glory "God's wisdom" (1 Cor 2:7). Like the teacher(s) of the Essene sect (1QH 12[= 4]:27), Paul can describe the apostles as persons who dispense these mysteries to others (1 Cor 4:1). Colossians 2:1-3 presents knowledge of the hidden mystery of God as part of the wisdom Christians attain through Paul's teaching. This mystery of salvation was hidden from prior ages but has been made manifest to the saints in Paul's preaching Christ among the Gentiles (Col 1:26-27).

The connection between revelation of the mystery and a preordained divine plan is firmly embedded in Essene writings (see 1QS 4:18-19, with reference to the future destruction of all evil). How-

ever, Ephesians lacks the interest in the succession of times characteristic of apocalyptic speculation that anticipates the end of the
present evil age by divine judgment (4 Ezra 4:37; 2 *Apoc. Bar.* 40:3;
81:4). As verse 10 suggests, the times have reached their fulfillment.
The term "plan" (Gk. *oikonomia*) has a range of meanings. The
primary secular meanings have to do with the management of a
household or city. An individual designated as *oikonomos* may be
the treasurer of a city (Rom 16:23), the estate administrator, or the
manager of a household. Often such persons were slaves with
considerable power over others, but other examples indicate that
freemen may have been administrators for extensive enterprises (see
Arion's administration of Hyrcannus's wealth in Josephus *Ant.* 12
§199-200; Spicq 1994). When "plan" is associated with God, it
refers to God's providential direction of all things in the cosmos.

The connection between the term "plan" and "the fullness of
time" (v. 10) suggests a temporal plan rather than a providential
ordering of the world. Paul used the expression "fullness of time"
for the coming of Jesus as redeemer from the Law and source of
Christian adoption as sons of God (Gal 4:4-5). That expression
designates a moment in the past that marked the transition from
divine promise to its fulfillment. But, as we have seen when Paul
uses the term "mystery" in Rom 11:25, he assumes that God's plan
of salvation has not been completed. First Corinthians 15:51-57
also uses "mystery" for future stages in the unfolding story of
salvation: subjection of all things to the Son, the bodily resurrection
of those who belong to Christ, and finally, the return of everything
to the Father. Does Ephesians assume that the exaltation of Christ
in the heavenly regions marks the end of all significant times of
salvation? Some argue that all the divine promises have been
realized and are present now in the experience of believers who
participate in the heavenly exaltation of Christ (so Lindemann
1975).

Ephesians appears to come down somewhere between anticipating a future stage of salvation and assuming that all salvation is
present in Christ. On the one hand, its eschatology departs from
common apocalyptic patterns in not anticipating any future critical
acts of salvation from God's side. The formulaic statement in verse

10*b* of what the fullness of time entails suggests more a static reality than a dynamic process. On the other hand, one cannot ignore the ongoing appropriation of the gospel by human beings.

Ephesians describes the "all things" gathered up in Christ in cosmic terms, all things in heaven and on earth. *How* all things are united in Christ is not specified at this point. Ephesians will develop that motif with the image of Christ as head of the cosmic body, the church ("somatic unity," Usami 1983). The confession of Christ's present power over the cosmos can be found in the ancient Christian hymn cited in Phil 2:9-11. Colossians 1:15-20 grounds its depiction of Christ's rule over all things in the role of the preexistent son of God in creation.

Ephesians continues in verses 11-12 with the benefits received by the elect. The expression "obtain an inheritance" evokes echoes of Israel's destiny to be God's "lot" or heritage (Deut 9:29). The Essenes frequently used this expression to describe their community (1QS 4:26; 11:7). Ephesians makes the risen Christ the basis for Christians to obtain their inheritance. It agrees with the Essenes that the elect have been called to praise God. Compare the Essene hymn, "I shall bless him for (his) great marvels and shall meditate on his power and shall rely on his compassion" (1QS 10:16). The concluding phrase in this section, "we, who were the first to set our hope on Christ," has led some scholars to suggest that the author has shifted to the perspective of the Jewish Christian "we" found in 2:11–3:6. (Gordon Fee [1994] notes a typical Pauline telegraphing of a theme in the body of the letter.) In that case, the phrase would employ the ambiguity of the Greek word *christos:* it can mean both "Christ" (a specific reference to Jesus) and "messiah" (the object of Jewish hopes). The next verse appears to contrast the "we" of this verse with the "you" of the Gentile readers. However, Ephesians has not yet introduced the Jew and Gentile distinction. Nor is such a division appropriate to the genre that draws speaker and audience together in praise of its subject.

One might treat the switch to "you" in verse 13 as a rhetorical way of drawing the audience into the act of praising God (so Lincoln 1990). Since the audience's tacit participation is, however, presumed by the genre, another explanation would seem to be required. The verse alludes to the audience's conversion upon hearing the preaching of the gospel. This mission terminology drawn from the earlier Pauline writings (Col 1:5; Rom 10:14-17) distinguishes the speaker from the audience. Paul is the agent through whom the gospel comes to be known. The "we" of verse 12 would refer to Paul. The Essenes also combine the language of truth revealed through their teacher(s) with an initiation that includes knowledge of the mysteries of God, forgiveness of sin and cleansing by God's Spirit (1QS 4:18-22).

The combination of "sealing" and "down payment" (NRSV: "pledge") with reference to the Spirit appears in 2 Cor 1:21-22. Though sealing would later become part of the baptismal rite (2 Clem. 7:6; 8:6; Herm. Sim. viii 6.3; ix 16.3-6), there is no evidence for those associations in 2 Cor 1:21-22 or Eph 1:13. However, the Essene example mentioned above does tie purification by "lustral waters" with the cleansing power of God's Spirit. The phrase "Holy Spirit of the promise" (NRSV: "the promised Holy Spirit") has inverted Gal 3:14, "promise of the Spirit." There the promise to Abraham has been received through faith in Christ. If the Spirit itself is understood to be the content of the promise, Old Testament passages that refer to the presence of God's Spirit in the last days serve as the basis for the expression (see Ezek 36:26-27; 37:14; Joel 2:28-30). Commentators who see the "you" of verse 13 as Gentiles who have been incorporated into the faith of the Jewish believers treat the Spirit as evidence that the promise of Jew and Gentile joined together is being fulfilled (Fee 1994). This reading reflects the theological use of Spirit and promise in Gal 3:14. If the "we"/"you" contrast between verses 12 and 13 is not read as referring to Jewish and then Gentile believers respectively, then there is little reason to explicate this expression as a theological account for the election of the Gentiles. The language suits poetic celebrations of divine election similar to that in Essene sources.

Although Ephesians depicts the gifts of salvation as fully present in the lives of believers, the designation "pledge" suggests a future perfection to this experience. A Semitic loan word, pledge (Gk. arrabōn) is used in commercial texts for "security, guarantee, or deposit." The translation "pledge" (NRSV) would be misleading if it suggested a legal promise to fulfill a commitment that establishes a human right against God. Rather, the deposit indicates that one has already received part of what has been promised to secure future delivery. Throughout the eulogy, Ephesians emphasizes the abundance of divine graciousness (vv. 3, 6, 8). The congruence between present and future salvation is reenforced by the phrase that specifies inheritance, "toward redemption as God's own people" (lit. "toward redemption of his possession"). Verse 7 indicated that believers have "redemption" from sin through the death of Christ. The meaning of "possession" (NRSV: "God's own people") in verse 14 is contested. If taken as a nominal form that designates an action, it would mean "the possessing." The expression might then be a shorthand reference to believers taking possession of their inheritance. However, the word can also be used to refer to a possession, in this case, the people as God's possession (LXX Mic 3:17; 1 Pet 2:9; Acts 20:28; so NRSV).

In keeping with the genre of praising a benefactor, the expression might refer to God redeeming his (or Christ's) possession. The benefits experienced by the speakers in the present will continue to characterize their lives. Their experience of the Spirit guarantees this relationship. God is, and will continue to be, the redeemer of the people. Finally, the eulogy concludes with the human response to divine graciousness, praise of God's glory (v. 14c).

◊ ◊ ◊ ◊

The compressed, poetic style of the opening eulogy suggests a number of theological themes without providing a conceptual development for any of them. The linguistic and metaphoric parallels from the Old Testament, Jewish and non-Jewish writings of the Greco-Roman period, and from the earlier Pauline letters, provide hints as to what first-century Christian audiences may have brought to their understanding of each phrase. It is easy to apprehend the dynamic involvement of God with human destiny that runs through this section. Its language of election embraces all things in a divine plan that existed before anything came into being. Despite their minority status in the world of first-century CE Asia Minor, Christians found themselves the center of God's cosmic design because they belonged to the risen Lord who is exalted over all of the heavenly powers. Benefits that humans might expect to receive from "the heavens" have been conferred by God in Christ.

We have seen that Ephesians adopted images that were suited to the cosmic picture of its age. The simpler Old Testament imagery of a heavenly dome over the earth was replaced by a multiplicity of heavenly regions. God's power operates through all of them. The "mystery" of God's plan invites believers to recognize that all things in the cosmos are brought together in the risen Christ. Ancient readers would readily think of a divine force behind the observed motions of the cosmos. Ancient audiences could imagine the arduous journey of the soul beyond the regions of the earth and moon through the spheres to the divine heavens (see M. R. Wright 1995).

Ephesians is making a claim about the universe as Paul's readers know it. The imagery of heavenly regions is not merely decoration for asserting the powerful sovereignty of God. Anyone who could journey like an apocalyptic visionary to the most distant regions of the universe would find God's creative and saving power at work to gather all things into Christ. Ephesians is not interested in a divine plan that was simply programmed into the creation of the universe as some Stoic cosmologies envisaged the multiple formations of a divine, rational spirit generating the universe. For Ephesians, the providential action of divine power is oriented forward, toward a redemption that brings all things in the cosmos together in Christ.

The dilemma of God's presence to believers in a vast universe was eloquently framed by Augustine. The God who is inside us, closer than we are to ourselves, is also "outside," quite beyond our comprehension. We cannot reach God without God having come toward us. Citing Joel 2:28, Augustine comments on the conceptual dilemma of divine presence: "When you are 'poured out' (see Joel 2:28) upon us, you are not wasted on the ground. You raise us upright. You are not scattered but reassemble us. In filling all things, you fill them all with the whole of yourself" (*Confes.* 1.3 (3); Augustine 1992, 4). Augustine also recognized that the distinction between God as creator and human creatures is essential to the dynamic of praise. Ephesians indicates that the purpose of our election is to praise God's glory. We cannot engage in that praise without the ability to perceive God's redeeming power at work.

Ephesians uses the language of divine election to describe the experience of God's grace touching the lives of believers. In this context, it is important to note the difference between Ephesians and the linguistic background provided by the Essene writings. Unlike the Qumran texts, Ephesians does not depict election as the division between a few righteous and the majority of human beings who are alienated from God. Instead, Ephesians sees redemption as the purpose that God has embedded in creation as a whole. Though Ephesians recognizes the human need for redemption from sin, its imagery suggests that God would have brought all things together in Christ even if Adam had not sinned. Forgiveness enables the elect to live before God in the holiness to which they are called (1:4).

THANKSGIVING PRAYER REPORT (1:15-23)

The thanksgiving of Pauline letters often signals themes taken up in what follows. The second, long periodic sentence in Ephesians serves that function. Ephesians combines phrases from Colossians (1:3-4, 9, 18) with its own emphasis on knowledge of God's saving power in Christ to create its thanksgiving. Rhetorically, the thanksgiving can be a way of gaining the goodwill of one's audience. The eulogy joined author and audience in the praise of their common benefactor, God (v. 13). Now the thanksgiving assures Christians who had not known the apostle Paul, that their reputation for faith and love has won them a place in his prayers. Paul used a similar strategy in addressing Christians in Rome, whom he had not yet visited (Rom 1:8-15).

The Thanksgiving falls into three sections: (a) the formal thanksgiving and prayer report (vv. 15-16); (b) the content of Paul's intercession (vv. 17-19); and (c) a christological expansion on God's energizing power in the exalted Christ (vv. 20-23). The intercessory report asks for insight and wisdom (vv. 17-19). The content of that knowledge returns to phrases from the eulogy: (a) spirit, wisdom, revelation, and one's ability to "come to know" in verse 17 echo the wisdom, insight, and making "known to us the mystery" of verses 8-9; (b) hope, riches, and inheritance in verse 18 pick up the earlier "first to set our hope" (v. 12), wealth (v. 7), and inheritance (v. 14).

Many commentators detect a hymnic formula describing the exaltation of Christ in verses 20-21, which has been expanded by a scriptural proof text (Ps 110:1) and its application to the Christ and the church. Emphasis on the role of the church in God's plan (v. 22) is an addition peculiar to Ephesians. The combination of Ps 110:1 and Ps 8:6 describes the eschatological triumph of the Lord independently of ecclesial imagery elsewhere in the New Testament (see 1 Cor 15:25-27; Heb 2:8-9; Dunn 1980, 108-9). The image of the risen Christ as head of the church derives from Col 1:18. The puzzling concluding clause (v. 23c), "the fullness of him who fills all in all," reformulates the mystery of God's plan from verse 10.

◊ ◊ ◊ ◊

15-16: The prayer report combines Col 1:3-4 and Phlm 4-5. Pauline thanksgivings make it clear that the appropriate response to evangelization is a reputation for Christian faith. The apostle's preaching would not be successful if his churches did not become known to others as places of faith and mutual love (see 1 Thess 1:3-12).

17-19: The thanksgiving modulates into the prayer wish for the readers in verses 17-19. The theocentric focus of the eulogy continues. A key element in the praise of God was "glory" (vv. 12, 14). This emphasis leads to a reformulation of the title for God. The earlier "Father of our Lord Jesus Christ" (v. 3) becomes "God of our Lord Jesus Christ" and "Father of glory" (v. 17a). The phrase "Father of glory" is not a common expression for God. Paul refers to Jesus as "the Lord of glory" in 1 Cor 2:8. The phrase "God of glory" occurs in Ps 28:3 (LXX) where "glory" is associated with the storm-god theophany tradition. James 1:17 refers to the "Father of lights" as the source of every good gift, a sentiment similar to that in Eph 1:3.

The initial content of the petition also reminds readers of the earlier emphasis on wisdom and knowledge of God's plan (vv. 8-9; 17b). Given the earlier reference to believers as being "marked with the seal of the promised Holy Spirit" (v. 13), the expression "spirit of wisdom" probably intends more than human perception of divine wisdom. God's Spirit is the source of all wisdom and knowledge among the elect. The author is not thinking of particular charismatic gifts that are only possessed by some members of the community, such as the special insight possessed by the apostle (3:3, 5).

Verse 18 describes the result of wisdom as "the eyes of your heart enlightened." This expression resembles the Essene language of election as in the blessing pronounced over those who enter the covenant, "May he illuminate your heart with the discernment of life and grace you with eternal knowledge," (1QS 2:3). By the second century, baptism was commonly described as enlightenment (so Justin Martyr *1 Apol.* 61.12; 65.1; *Dial. Trypho* 39.2; 122.1, 2, 6). Ephesians 4:18 speaks of Gentiles who do not know God as "darkened in their understanding." The addressees are warned not to return to that state. Ephesians treats the darkness to light image as a reference to the moral conversion associated with turning to God. The fact that individuals might revert to darkness shows that illumination of the heart is not a transformation that becomes permanent as soon as someone becomes a Christian.

Although the Old Testament regularly uses "heart" for the seat of human understanding (Ps 10:11; Prov 2:2), the phrase "eyes of your heart" has no biblical antecedents. However, Prov 20:27 (LXX) speaks of the breath of humans as the light of the Lord searching out hidden storerooms of the belly. Other Jewish texts refer to the darkened or clouded eye as equivalent to a depraved will (*T. Iss.* 4:6; *T. Benj.* 4:2; see Spicq 1994). These examples suggest that the expression "eyes of your heart" is associated with change in conduct. Greek moralists may have contributed to such expressions. Matthew 6:22-23 also refers to an "eye" that is healthy and one that is evil or diseased. This saying refers to the inner light required for ethical discernment. Platonic and Stoic philosophers commonly link that light with reason. Matthew challenges the philosophic assumption that humans can rely on such inner light, since the eye can be darkened (Betz 1995, 84-87).

The content of enlightenment reiterates earlier statements about Christian hope (v. 18*b*, *c*; 14*a*). Since the passage speaks of "his [= God's] glorious inheritance," some commentators presume that the meaning of "saints" (Gk. *hagioi*) has shifted from "saints" as God's elect to "saints" as "the holy ones," that is, angels (so Deut 33:2-3; Ps 89:6, 8; Dan 8:13). On this reading, Ephesians would be similar to the Essene writings in claiming that the heritage of the elect lies with the angelic hosts (Schnackenburg 1991; see 1QS 11:7-8). Against this interpretation of verse 18, verse 15 has used "saints" for those who are fellow Christians within the audience.

Verse 19 shifts from knowledge of one's place among God's elect to recognition of the power of God at work in those who believe. An echo of Col 1:11, the phrase is replete with words for power. The author does not focus on the cosmological manifestations of divine power (as in 1QS 11:18-19, for example). Just as the eulogy's account of God's activity in creation (vv. 3-5) was not cosmological but soteriological, so verse 19 describes the power of God as "for us who believe." Verse 19*b* shifts from "you" (plural) to the inclusive "we" in order to set up the parallelism between God's work in the believer and what God has done in raising Christ (v. 20; Gnilka 1980).

The expression "working of his great power" connects verse 19*b* with 20*a*. Some interpreters treat it as the introduction to the next section (Lincoln 1990). Colossians 1:29*b* speaks of God's powerful energy at work in the struggles of Paul's ministry. Colossians 2:12 speaks of God's power [= "energy"] to raise the dead. Since Ephesians uses expressions associated with divine energy and power to connect God's activity within believers and the resurrection of Christ, the phrase may be derived from earlier Christian formulae.

20-23: The concluding section of this chapter (vv. 20-23) is widely recognized as the development of a credal formula. Attempts to isolate the specific words of a hymn have not been persuasive (Lincoln 1990). Verse 20 alludes to the ancient tradition of resurrection as heavenly exaltation at God's right hand (Dan 12:2-3; Phil 2:9-11; Acts 2:32-33). The audience already knows that Christ serves to mediate God's gracious blessings from the heavens (v. 3).

Ephesians treats the exaltation of Jesus rather than the cross as the focus of God's saving power (Barth and Blanke 1994, 169). Paul links the resurrection of Jesus and divine power in contexts that contrast resurrection with the cross (Rom 1:4; 1 Cor 6:14; 2 Cor 13:4; Phil 3:10). Ephesians may have shifted the traditional emphasis in order to highlight the permanent victory of God's power.

Hellenistic Jewish court tales celebrated exaltation as the victory of a righteous sage over the enemy (see Dan 1–6). Daniel 7:13-27 depicts a human figure ascending to God's throne. With his ascent comes vindication for the righteous and eternal dominion for the "holy ones of the Most High" (Dan 7:27). With the corporate interpretation of the heavenly figure as representative of the righteous, Dan 7:13-27 provides a key to the connection between heavenly exaltation of a figure to God's throne and the eventual triumph of God's elect. This apocalyptic scenario also includes two other elements that are represented in Ephesians: (a) use of the "holy ones" (Dan 7:18, 21, 25, 27) in a way that could refer to the righteous or the angelic hosts (Collins 1993) and (b) exaltation as victory over powers that threaten human and divine order (Dan 7:23-25).

The exaltation Christology of Ephesians requires that Christ be superior to all the heavenly powers (v. 21). The text does not indicate whether the reader should consider this catalogue of powers as hostile (so Daniel) or angelic (so Heb 1:3-4). Colossians 1:16 associates a list of powers with the affirmation that the cosmos was created in Christ, "whether thrones or dominions or rulers or powers" (Gk. *exousia*). Ephesians 1:21*a* omits "thrones" and includes *dynamis* (NRSV: "power"; for Gk. *exousia* the NRSV shifts to "authority"). Similar lists in apocalyptic texts can be associated with angels (see 1 *Enoch* 61:10; 2 *Enoch* [J] 20:1; T. *Levi* 3:8) or with Satan's cohorts (*Ascen. Is.* 2:2). Ephesians concludes the list of powers with the statement that Christ has the name above every name. This topos appears elsewhere in early christological formulae (see Phil 2:9-11, "Lord"; Heb 1:4-5, "Son"). The concluding phrase (v. 21*c*) evokes the apocalyptic picture of present and future ages. Just as the Son of Man and the holy ones in Dan 7:13-27 receive an eternal dominion, so the exalted Christ enjoys eternal rule. This affirmation raises a theological question when this passage is compared with Paul's account in 1 Cor 15:23-28. There the Second Coming will be needed to complete the Son's domination of all the powers. At that point, Christ will hand dominion over to the Father. Though Ephesians focuses on the Father in its depiction of divine power, the author does not anticipate a "handing over" of the kingdom to God.

The scenario in Ephesians cannot be squared with the historical perspective of apocalypses like Daniel, which correlate heavenly or symbolic figures with political powers. In such historical apocalypses no claim to dethrone hostile powers could be sustained without the corresponding defeat of evil in its socio-political manifestations. The significance of language about Christ's exaltation over the powers in Colossians and Ephesians remains contested. Ephesians refers to an angelic leader of the hostile powers (2:2; 6:11). If the powers of this list are hostile, then Christ is a victorious conqueror (Schnackenburg 1991). Others have highlighted the reference to Christ's superior name. They suggest that Ephesians is concerned with the use of angelic names in magical texts. The Christ whose name is superior to those of any such powers has rendered the powers of magic impotent (Arnold 1989). When Ephesians is read over against the ideology of the Roman emperor cult, its encomium to the exalted Christ (especially 2:11-22) appears to copy the style of speeches in praise of the emperor (Faust 1993).

Identification of the list of powers with causes of socio-political or individual evil presumes that the powers in this list are the demonic powers referred to later in Ephesians. Since the eulogy and the thanksgiving both depend upon traditional, formulaic phrases for divine blessing, the positive use of angelic powers and name formulae in christological acclamations and hymns seems to be more appropriate in this section. God has made all things subject to the risen and exalted Lord (1 Cor 15:25). That same power will be effective in the resurrection of the faithful (Phil 3:21).

In the earlier Pauline letters, references to the future completion of salvation indicate that the present subjection of all things remains a stage in an ongoing process: (a) Christ turns all things over to the Father (1 Cor 15:28); (b) believers are transformed into the image of the risen one (Phil 3:21). Unlike these examples, Ephesians remains focused on the present evidence of salvation. Verse 22*b* takes from Ps 110:1 the image of Christ as head over the universal church, "he has put all things under his feet." This motif picks up the earlier statement that God's preordained plan was to bring all things together in Christ (v. 10). Ephesians consistently uses "church" in the universal sense found in Colossians (1:18, 24).

In 1 Cor 12:12-27 (and Rom 12:4-5) Paul adopts a common philosophical image for the political community as a body in which each has an assigned role. Differences in status, activity, and power are necessary for the well-being of the whole. Paul's appropriation of this image to promote concord in the Corinthian community also fits common philosophical usage (Tacitus *Annals* 1.12, 13; Plutarch *Life of Galba* 4.3; Philo *Spec. Leg.* 1.210; Cicero *Off.* 1.25.85). Colossians 1:18 has universalized the image by alluding to philosophical traditions that transferred the communal sense of "body" to the harmonious coordination of the cosmos. The universe was considered to be a living being. Hence the move to describing it as a body was not as great as it would be for today's readers (for example Plato *Timaeus* 30B-34B; 47C-48B; Cicero *Nat. Deor.* 1.35; 3.9; Seneca *Ira* 2.31.7,8). For Colossians, the image of Christ as head of the body makes a natural transition between the creation of all things in Christ and the church that comes into being through the death and resurrection of Jesus.

Ephesians has adopted the imagery of Colossians for a different purpose—to express the completeness of salvation. Christ's superiority to the powers of the cosmos makes the existence of the church possible. However, Ephesians distinguishes the subjection of the powers from the function of Christ as head of the church. Christ is not a distant potentate ruling the church (Usami 1983). The concluding description of the "body" as "fullness" involves several exegetical difficulties. Is "fullness" in apposition to "body" or to Christ (as in Col 1:19; 2:9)? In Ephesians, "fullness" makes better grammatical sense as a reference to the body.

The meaning of the term "fullness" is more problematic. Elaborate discussions of a divine "fullness" as the goal of salvation appear in Gnostic writings from the second and third centuries CE. There "fullness" refers to the realm of divine light that is permanently separated from the darkness, chaos, and evil of this world. A primordial fall led to elements of that light being held captive in this world by the rulers of the planetary spheres (often equated with the OT God). Christ, or some other redeemer figure, must break into this world in order to provide the souls that possess light with the means to return to the "fullness" (for example *Gos. Truth* 41,1-16; *Ap. John* 30,16). Gnostic texts often suggest that when all the light has been restored the "deficiency," that is, the lower world, vanishes (Evans 1984). However, Ephesians shows no evidence of the Gnostic dualism (Fischer 1973). Therefore, it is more probable that Ephesians has taken the term from a hymnic tradition like Col 1:19.

The noun "fullness" can have an active sense ("that which fills") or a passive sense ("that which is filled"); it can also refer to the activity of filling. In the Old Testament the noun is used in the active sense (Pss 95:11; 23:1; 49:12; Jer 8:6; Ezek 12:19; 19:7; 30:12). Ephesians 1:23 echoes Old Testament descriptions of God or a divine attribute filling all things (Jer 23:23, 24 [LXX]; Isa 6:3; Wis 1:7; 7:24). Later in the Epistle, both Christ (4:10) and the Spirit (5:18) are agents of filling. Since Eph 4:10 refers to the ascent of Christ above the heavens in order to fill the universe, the phrase, "fullness of him who fills all in all" probably belongs to the same tradition. Nothing remains outside the Christ who fills all (Lincoln 1990). Ephesians does not indicate how the church as Christ's fullness is related to his presence to all things.

◊ ◊ ◊ ◊

The ecclesial conclusion of the thanksgiving sounds a motif that will reappear in the letter. Christ's body, the church, experiences the divine life and power of God that fills all things. Readers sometimes assume that the equation between the church and "fullness" is a call to action, that the Christian mission is responsible for filling the world with Christ. Ephesians does not identify the church with the "all things" of the cosmos. Instead, without explaining how the two activities of "filling" are related, this section of Ephesians suggests a special relationship between the church and Christ by using the image of head and body.

The opening of the thanksgiving period gave a more conventional picture of the addressees as the community of the elect. They have become known to others as a community that has faith in the Lord Jesus and demonstrates that faith in love. They believe that the risen Lord has been exalted at God's right hand and have experienced God's power in their lives. When the prayer report turns to imagery of the cosmic power of Christ, Ephesians moves beyond the world as structured by human powers and communities to a world that includes the heavens and ranks of angelic (or demonic) powers. Verse 21 insists that Christ has the name greater than any other, not only in the present age but in the future. Whether involved in magical practices or not, many persons in the first century CE would have agreed that proper knowledge of angelic or magical names was critical to one's life. Magicians could use the knowledge of such names to enlist the aid of cosmic powers. Angelic powers might be named to facilitate the soul's journey into the heavens either at death or as part of a mystical vision. For the apocalyptic visions of the rise and fall of earthly rulers, the angelic or demonic figures behind the human community were also perceived as a real threat. Consequently, the vision of Christ's exaltation found in Ephesians removes believers from the influence of all other powers.

The lists of powers in Colossians-Ephesians aim to embrace all forces that are thought to control humans and events in the cosmos. Since neither angelic nor magical names are used, the claims made for God's effective power in the risen Christ are not wedded to a particular mythological scenario. A modern list of cosmic powers could be substituted for the ancient examples (Barth and Blanke 1994, 202). Perhaps the ambiguity over whether the powers are demonic or angelic was also deliberate. Ephesians intends to fold all "powers" in the cosmos into the power of God expressed through the exalted Christ. Christians should not assume that other powers in the cosmos, or in the political order, stand between them and salvation. Nor do other powers contribute positive benefits to human life.

The "filling" already exists as a divine reality (v. 23). Christians are not subject to powers that must be overcome as was the case for those who thought that heavenly powers stood between the soul and salvation in the heavens. If Christians recognize the presence and power of God in all things, they have a secure basis for the hope for the "riches of [God's] glorious inheritance" (v. 18). The theology of election in Ephesians reminds Christians that God is the source of their hope and faith. Hope as a Christian virtue is not a psychological trait but a response to what God is (Conzelmann 1985).

Finally, Ephesians challenges the tendency to define the church from the perspective of its existence as a socio-political institution. It stands the earlier Pauline usage of church on its head. The local assemblies to which the earlier letters refer have given place to the cosmic vision of church as a divine reality. The "body" image was used for both socio-political entities and for the universe as a whole. Consequently, Ephesians builds on the earlier tradition in order to expand the vision of church from local to cosmic community.

Since Ephesians shows no signs of the Gnostic dualism between the divine realm and the material world, the "fullness" of the body is not limited to the heavenly realm where Christ is exalted. Ancient thinkers who depicted the divine spirit or wisdom pervading the universe (as in Philo *Leg.* 3.4) presumed that this spirit had a natural affinity with human intellectual and spiritual capacities. Ephesians rejects the view that human knowledge of God is part of creation as such. It is received as divine gift. The shift from cosmological to soteriological imagery highlights another central conviction of this letter: redemption belonged to the divine plan prior to creation. Unlike Gnostic myth, creation is not a hostile trap for light that belongs to the divine world. It is oriented toward salvation that comes in Christ. Knowledge of God comes with the conversion of human understanding through revelation (vv. 17-18).

BODY OF THE LETTER (2:1–6:20)

Theological Reflection on Salvation in the Body of the Exalted Christ (2:1–3:21)

From Death to New Life (2:1-10)

The body of the letter picks up the "you" and "us" of 1:18-19 in a long Greek sentence that the NRSV has divided into three sentences (vv. 1-2, 3, 4-7). The section shifts from the Gentile past of the letter's audience, "you," to the experience of salvation shared by all Christians, "we." The expression, "by grace you have been saved" (v. 5c) returns in the conclusion of this section, which also moves from "you" (vv. 8-9) to "we" (v. 10).

The Greek sentence in verses 1-7 divides into two halves, each beginning with a plural pronoun and a variation of the phrase "being dead in trespasses" (vv. 1, 5). The first half begins with "you" and contains a lengthy expansion on sins that then incorporate "us" (v. 3) in the story of sin and grace (v. 4). The second half continues with the "us" from verses 3-4 and depicts salvation as being raised to the heavens (v. 6). The "you" of the first half of the sentence reappears in a parenthetical phrase in verse 5b, "by grace you have been saved." This phrase returns in the next sentence (vv. 8-9) to anchor a Pauline "faith not works" contrast. Verse 10 returns to the "we" who are predestined to good works. Since the sentence divisions of verses 1-7 in the NRSV do not fit the grammatical structure of the Greek sentence, the commentary reflects the NRSV by treating verses 1-3 and verses 4-7 as separate sections.

Grammatically, the "you" and "we" of verses 1 and 3 are objects of God's action. The subject of the Greek sentence (vv. 1-7) is not mentioned until verse 4. "God, who is rich in mercy" is the agent of new life and exaltation. The adjective "rich" in verse 4 and the "riches of his grace" in verse 7 provide a link to the previous sections: "riches of his grace" (1:7) and "riches of his glorious inheritance" (1:18). Thus, the opening section stresses the graciousness of God's life-giving power, not the sinfulness of life without God.

Three negative statements are reversed in the event of salvation (Bouttier 1991): (a) dead through trespasses (vv. 1, 5), made alive in Christ (v. 5); (b) living according to passions (v. 3), risen with Christ (v. 6); (c) subject to a demonic power (v. 2 [v. 3b, treating "children of wrath" as equivalent to "those who are disobedient"]), seated in the heavenly regions with Christ (v. 6). Romans 6:1-14 uses a number of "with" compounds to insist that Christians no longer live under sin or the passions of the body (vv. 12-14): crucified with, died with, buried with, live with. There "raised" lacks the "with" prefix when applied to believers. For Romans, being in the risen Christ remains for the future (6:8). Colossians 2:10-13 attaches similar verbs to a concrete issue: that Christians are free from physical circumcision through baptism—by being buried with, raised with, and made alive with Christ (vv. 12-13). Ephesians may have derived its language of conversion from these two passages. Although Colossians combines Christ's victory over the powers with the Christian's present participation in resurrection, there is no parallel to the co-enthronement language of Eph 2:6. The exhortation to set the mind on "things that are above, where Christ is" in Col 3:1-2 avoids placing Christians "in the heavens." Ephesians removes all spatial and temporal separation between believers and the exalted Christ by including "seated us with him in the heavenly places" (v. 6) as a consequence of conversion.

◊ ◊ ◊ ◊

1-3: The author turns to address his audience. The connection between sin and death (v. 1) is characteristic of the Pauline tradition (Rom 5:12-21; 1 Cor 15:56; Col 2:13). The Essenes also describe persons who join the sect as raised from the "worms of the dead" to the "lot of your holy ones" (1QH 19[= 11]:10-14).

Verse 2 introduces a familiar apocalyptic topos: all who are not among the elect belong to a sinful humanity inspired by a demonic angelic power. The designation, "sons of disobedience" (NRSV: "those who are disobedient"), exhibits a pattern familiar from the Essene writings: "sons of darkness" (1QS 1:10; 1QM 1:7, 16), "sons of deceit" (1QS 3:21), "sons of guilt" (1QH 13[= 5]:7). An angelic power inspires the evil deeds that human beings do: "in the hand of the Angel of Darkness is total dominion over the sons of deceit; they walk on paths of darkness" (1QS 3:20-21).

The two "following the course of" clauses attached to "you once lived" are unclear. The expression "course of this world" combines a temporal word, *aiōn* ("course"; translated "age" in 1:21; 2:7), and a spatial one, *world* (1:4; 2:12). Since Gnostic sources often used the term *"aiōn"* for the spiritual beings associated with levels of the heavenly "fullness," interpreters who see Gnostic influence in Ephesians treat *aiōn* as a spiritual being. This reading makes the two clauses variants of each other (Gnilka 1980). However, to fit the Gnostic examples, *aiōn* could not be used to describe this world. For example, the hostile Jewish God is described as "god, the archon of the aeons and powers" (*Apoc. Adam* 64,20-26) or as "the archon of the powers" (*Hyp. Arch.* 92,8-10). The Johannine expression, "archon of this world" (12:31; 16:11; NRSV: "ruler") is the expression one would expect of a spiritual power responsible for evil (also see 1 Cor 2:6, 8; 2 Cor 4:4, "god of this aeon"; NRSV: "god of this world").

Since *aiōn* is consistently used as a temporal term in Pauline writings and elsewhere in Ephesians, it should have that meaning here (Lincoln 1990). The NRSV obscured the difficulties in the text by translating the phrase "course of this world." That expression is too neutral. When either an apocalyptic or a Pauline text refers to "this age," the assumption is that the evil powers that dominate the present age are under divine judgment. For the Essenes, the present time involves conflict between those who follow paths of truth and those who do deeds of injustice. God's plan will bring that situation to an end. "There exists a violent conflict in respect of all his decrees since they do not walk together. God in the mysteries of his knowledge and the wisdom of his glory, has determined an end to injustice and on the occasion of his visitation he will obliterate it forever," (1QS 4:17-19).

Ephesians has not developed the dualism found in such apocalyptic writings, but the imagery in this section echoes apocalyptic language. Therefore "*aiōn*" must refer to the temporal span of this world as limited by God's judgment. The second "following" clause clearly refers to a demonic figure responsible for evil. Unlike the Essene writings that depict a dualistic struggle in the hearts of humans between the Angel of Darkness and the Prince of Lights (1QS 3:20-21), Ephesians highlights the overwhelming power of God. Since Christ is above every "authority" (1:21), the ruler of such powers has no authority over believers.

Gnostic mythology embedded the triumph over the powers in a mythological reading of the Genesis story. The evil archon whose power is shattered by the coming of the revealer is the God of

Genesis. When awakened to their divine nature, the Gnostic descendants of the spiritual Adam and Eve can laugh at the vain attempts of the archon and his powers to govern the elect. For example, *Hyp. Arch.* has the Gnostic ancestress, Norea, confront the chief of the archons with the defiant words: "It is you who are the rulers of darkness who are accursed.... For I am not your descendant; rather it is from the world above that I am come" (92,22-26). The introduction to this tractate in the fourth-century codex tells the recipient that he has copied it because of an inquiry about the reality of the powers described by the apostle in phrases taken from Col 1:13 and Eph 6:12. Even in antiquity, Gnostic myths were used to provide clues to the cosmological soteriology of Ephesians.

However, this same text shows what is not gnosticizing about Ephesians. The key lies in the description of the ruler as governing the "power of the air." The region of the "air" continues the engagement with popular hellenistic cosmology evident in the expression "heavenly regions" (Bouttier 1991). "Air" is the murky, polluted region between the planet earth and the moon in which the four elements (earth, water, air, and fire) are mixed (Barton 1994). In some accounts, the visible universe is divided into three regions connected to each of the four elements: (a) stars and sun are linked with fire; (b) the moon with air; and (c) the earth with water (Plutarch *Fac.* 943F [citing Xenocrates]). Ancient writers regularly argued that "demons," in the neutral sense of spiritual beings, must occupy the air. Philo treats the *daimones* as both beneficent agents of God and as evil angels (Philo *Gig.* 8-18). Plutarch's teacher Ammonius, whose views also appear in Philo (*Quaes. Gen.* 4.8), developed Plato's demiurge into a lower power that rules the sublunary world. This power was also designated Hades or Pluto (Dillon 1977, 169-70).

To a first-century reader familiar with such cosmology, Eph 2:2 attributes human sinfulness to the rulers of the sublunary region. Read in astrological terms, the connection between phases of the moon and the passions would provide an explanation for the action of the lower powers. Firmicus says that horoscopes that have the waning moon in relation to mercury indicate a particularly malicious character: "They willingly associate themselves with all kind of wickedness, defend evil men and evil deeds, and their depravity increases from day to day; they are even hostile to men of their own kind" (*Mathēsis* 5.6.10). The parallel formulation in Eph 2:3 refers to those trapped in sin as following the desires or urgings of "flesh" and "thoughts" (*dianoiōn*; NRSV: "senses"). As the astrological example demonstrates, planetary forces work on both the physical body and the ideas in an individual's mind. The term "spirit" in verse 2 has no connection with references to God's "spirit" elsewhere in Ephesians. Popular Stoic defenses of astrology used the all-pervading "spirit" as an explanation of how astrological influences are transmitted (Barton 1994, 104).

Some interpreters see the combination of hellenistic cosmology and Jewish apocalyptic imagery of verses 1-3 as a demonizing of the "neutral" (though not always beneficent) powers that would imply that a personal power of evil is at work in leading people into sin (Lincoln 1990). Ephesians assumes that disobedience means not walking in the paths established by God but does not require a cosmic being opposed to God in order to make that point. The letter derives its language about the universality of sin from Paul. The "we" links the sender with the audience in a past of alienation from God. God's wrath (Eph 5:6; Col 3:5, 6) belongs to the demonstration of divine righteousness in Paul (Rom 1:18, 25; 3:5; 4:15; 5:9; 9:22; 12:19; 13:4, 5). The comments on grace and works in verses 8-9 recall Paul's discussion of the Law, but unlike Paul, Ephesians uses "righteousness" only in a conventional, moral sense as the opposite of "sin." This letter sees no need to defend the possibility of righteousness apart from the Law, a central problem of Paul's theology.

Verse 3c asserts that "we . . . like everyone else" are subject to God's wrath "by nature." Sometimes Paul uses "nature" for the natural or created order (Rom 1:26; 1 Cor 11:14). In Gal 2:15, those who are Jewish "by nature," that is, by birth (as translated by the NRSV), are not sinners like Gentiles (and in a similar sense of Gentiles, Rom 2:27). Thus, though Paul can speak of all humans implicated in sin from the beginning (Rom 5:12-21), he would hardly describe the Jew as "child of wrath" by nature. Wisdom 13:1 exhibits the Jewish patterns of speech employed by the apostle.

Without the Law, human beings are by nature idolaters. The expression "by nature, children of wrath" fits the depiction of Gentile ignorance of God in Rom 1:18-32.

Romans 2:14-16 indicates that Gentiles who do not have the Law but perform its requirements "by nature" will be appropriately rewarded by God. Consequently, Paul does not use "nature" to describe a principle that separates humans from God. Use of Eph 2:3 as evidence for the doctrine of original sin belongs to later theological development. The formula in this passage must be based on the general Jewish tradition of Gentile sinfulness, even though the "we" includes Paul as a Jewish Christian (Schnackenburg 1991).

4-7: The subject of this section finally emerges in verse 4: God's graciousness toward those lost in sin. "Rich in mercy" and "love" were introduced as characteristics of God's actions toward us in the eulogy (1:5, 7-8) and thanksgiving (1:18). Elsewhere the expression "make alive with Christ" is embedded in Pauline descriptions of baptism (Rom 6:1-14; Col 2:11-13). Some interpreters think that readers would naturally understand a reference to baptism here. However Ephesians moves in a different direction. Its emphasis lies on the power of God evident in heavenly exaltation. The gift of life in verses 5-6 develops the christological vision of 1:19-23. The earlier passage described God's power; here it depicts God's love. In both instances, exaltation above the heavens with the risen Christ is the key to the Ephesians' understanding of salvation.

The three "with" expressions—"made alive with," "raised up with," and "seated with"—are interrupted by a parenthetical comment, "by grace you have been saved" (v. 5c). The same expression opens the next sentence (v. 8). Ephesians 1:7 attached the grace of God to a formulaic description of the cross as sin-offering. Since verses 1-3 described the past life of sin as "being dead," the parenthetical comment in verse 5 may be intended to remind readers of the fact that forgiveness of sin is central to "being made alive." It also suggests that the traditional Pauline juxtaposition of cross (dying with Christ) and resurrection (Rom 6:1-4) has not been completely erased by the emphasis on heavenly exaltation.

An Essene parallel to the exaltation of the righteous has been found in a scroll fragment that links exaltation and suffering (4Q521). The text speaks of God's saving activity toward the righteous, "and upon the poor he will place his spirit, and the faithful he will renew with strength. For he will honor *the devout upon the throne of eternal royalty* . . . and the Lord will perform marvellous acts such as have not existed, just as he sa[id] for he will heal the badly wounded and will *make the dead live*" (4Q521 Frag. 2 col. 2:6-7, 12; emphasis added). Ephesians makes the exaltation of the faithful a function of their identification with the exalted Christ (1:20-22). This relationship erases the temporal gap between the present in which the righteous live and their future glory.

Verse 7 provides an apparent reason for the heavenly exaltation of the righteous, to prove a point and "show . . . the immeasurable riches of his grace." The Greek expression translated "in the ages to come" by the NRSV could have a very different reading. Should the word *aiōn* ("age") be taken as a temporal term or as a reference to the powers that dominate human life? Ephesians 3:10 speaks of the manifestation of God's wisdom to the rulers and authorities in the heavenly places. If "*aiōns*" referred to powers, then this phrase would be a variant of 3:9-10 (Schlier 1957; Dibelius and Greeven 1953; Conzelmann 1985; Lindemann 1975). This understanding requires the participle *eperchomenos* to mean "attack" rather than the more usual meaning of "coming on" or "approaching." But several grammatical problems make this reading difficult.

The Greek verb "*endeiknumi*" (NRSV: "show") uses the preposition *eis* or the dative case for those to whom something is shown. However, this phrase begins with *en* ("in"). A temporal sense of *aiōn* combined with the usual meaning of "approaching" for the participle provides a grammatically acceptable reading, "in coming ages." Ephesians 2:7 extends the manifestation of salvation that has taken place in the exaltation of Christ (1:6-10), in the inheritance given the faithful (1:18-20), and in their exaltation with Christ (2:6) into the indefinite future.

8-10: The parenthetical reference from verse 5 to salvation by grace returns in verses 8-9 with a number of familiar Pauline expressions: grace (Rom 3:24; 11:6), faith (Gal 2:16), gift (Rom 3:24), boasting excluded by faith (Rom 3:27). The speaker shifts from "you" to addressing the audience as "we." Verse 8*b* underlines the fact that salvation is entirely God's gift, not the result of human effort. Verse 9 highlights that point by rejecting works. Though these expressions are easily expanded in light of Paul's theological controversies over the role of the Law, it is less clear why they are introduced at this point in Ephesians. Certainly, the Essene parallels to the language of election in the Epistle would have assumed that obedience to the Law is required for salvation. The shorthand "works" in verse 9 alludes to the Pauline "works of the Law" (Gal 2:16; 3:2-5, 9, 10; Rom 3:27-28; 4:2-5; 9:32; Rom 11:6 contrasts works and grace). However the parallel phrase in verse 8, "your own doing," allows a more general reading. An audience familiar with the conversion language of popular philosophical teachers might conclude that turning away from sin, the powers of the cosmos, can be accomplished by human efforts or human teaching.

This passage also departs from its Pauline antecedents in substituting "being saved" for Paul's justification. Grace prohibits boasting rather than the cross or justification through faith (as in Rom 3:27; 1 Cor 1:28-31). The "for" that attaches verse 10 to the preceding indicates a further explanation of why boasting is excluded. This sentence shifts back to the generalized "we" of verses 4-7. It also qualifies the apparent rejection of works in verse 9 by suggesting that the righteous have been elected to perform certain good works. The last phrase "be our way of life" provides an inclusion with the "you once lived" in verse 2.

Essene writings would agree that divine election is expressed in the "good works" of the righteous, walking according to God's decrees. But this view generally takes the form of predestination. The good works of the sons of light are contrasted with the works of those dominated by the spirit of injustice, "in agreement with man's birthright in justice and in truth, so he abhors injustice; and according his share in the lot of injustice he acts irreverently in it and so abhors the truth" (1QS 4:24). Though Paul rejects the idea that good works create the righteousness that will stand up in God's judgment, he can describe the moral conduct that God expects as "good work" (Rom 2:7; 13:3; 2 Cor 9:8; Col 1:9-10). The ethical exhortation that concludes Ephesians requires holy and blameless conduct. The thanksgiving opened with a reminder that the faith for which the Ephesians were known included love of one another. With its emphasis on the present reality of salvation, some readers might infer that ritual identification with the risen Christ or particular convictions about the powers of the cosmos form the core of Christian experience. Verse 10*b* points to the purpose of divine election, the good works that have also been preordained by God.

Verse 10*a* introduces the image of Christians as God's special creation. The Greek word for "what he has made us" *(poiēma)* is used in the LXX for creation as God's work (Pss 9:14; 14:25). It has the same sense in Rom 1:20. By itself the affirmation that "we are his [= God's] creation" could refer to God's original creation. Ephesians 1:4 described election to "holy and blameless" conduct as established before the creation. Since the next clause contains the phrase "created in Christ," though, most interpreters assume that Ephesians is not referring to the divine plan in creation, but to the Pauline "new creation" (Gal 6:15; 2 Cor 5:17). Galatians 6:15 uses "new creation" as the replacement for the divisive categories of Jew or Gentile. Ephesians may have introduced this expression as a link to the theme of the next section.

◊ ◊ ◊ ◊

The opening of the body of the letter continues the tone set by the eulogy and thanksgiving concerning God's salvation. The initial description of sin raises a question: What does it mean to speak of humans as trapped in sin or subject to a malevolent power? Traditional Christian theology understands all humans as subject to original sin. Taking "by nature" (v. 3) in the common sense of "by birth," humans are alienated from God and implicated in the sinfulness that began with Adam. A variant understanding appears in the Essene accounts of predestination. Though God is not directly responsible for the deeds of the wicked, God does permit the existence of the two conflicting powers and foreknows the existence of two "lots" of human beings. This predestination does not vitiate the need for God's grace among the righteous. They recognize that God's spirit enlightens, cleanses from sin, and sustains the life of holiness.

We have seen that Ephesians' use of "ruler of the power of air" to describe the force that governs the lives of sinners enabled its author to connect with cosmological speculation of its time. Augustine refers to Rom 7:7-25 as evidence that the irrational divisions of human willing are punishment for the sinful condition of humans in Adam (*Confes.* viii 9.21-10.22). He rejects the dualistic view of the Manichees that attributes such divisions to the conflict between good and evil powers (*Confes.* viii 10.24). This shift indicates the dangers of personifying the dualistic powers of apocalyptic. Individuals may conclude that they are not implicated in the works to which they have been predestined. Does Ephesians imply that human psychic and intellectual life is inherently distorted? Ephesians 2:3 treats the entire human person, bodily desires and mental life, as alienated from God. The dark side of this perspective hints that humans are not able to devise the needed "good works" on their own. Yet the dualism implied by such a reading conflicts with another motif in Ephesians, the close connection between the world that God created and salvation. As we have seen, verse 10 speaks of "us" as God's creation in a way that compresses both God's initial creation and redemption (Gnilka [1980] suggests references to the combination of the two in Col 1:15-20).

Ephesians has placed its description of sin in subordinate clauses. The focus of the opening period is God's grace and love experienced by the redeemed. That experience of God is not inherently known to human beings. Conversion implies turning away from a life in which God was absent. Ephesians uses the religious metaphors of its age in speaking of the past as "dead in sins" or as following the powers that govern the age and the lower world. By depicting believers alive, risen and exalted in the heavens with Christ, Ephesians breaks the sense that humans are constrained by a complex web of powers that are not under their control. When the question of evil arises, no Christian can claim that he or she had no choice but participate. God did not predestine his creatures to works of injustice but to good works.

Unity in Christ (2:11-22)

The "you" are now identified specifically as Gentiles, while the "we" belong to the "commonwealth of Israel." The "once but now" pattern applies to the prior division of the two groups, now brought together as one. Since the next section (3:1-21) depicts the apostle as the one who proclaimed this mystery, some interpreters treat 2:11–3:21 as a single section. However, Eph 3:1 marks a strong rhetorical transition by introducing the apostle's character. Therefore, it introduces a new section in the Epistle.

Alterations between, "you," "us both," and "you" divide this section into three parts: verses 11-13; verses 14-18; and verses 19-22. The middle section contains a number of formulaic phrases that have been described as fragments of an early Christian hymn (vv. 14-16; Wilhelmi 1987). This liturgical sounding piece has been combined with an echo of Isa 57:19 and applied to the argument (vv. 17-18). The catchword *peace* ties the two parts of this section together. A reference to the cross in verse 16*b* ties the midsection to the conclusion of the first "you" section (v. 13).

The final "you" section (vv. 19-22) introduces a new image for the community, the household of God. It highlights the results of becoming part of Christ by describing the dwelling of God as being built up. Antithetical parallels with the first "you" section make the second "you" section a response to the first (Bouttier 1991). Verse 11 speaks of the Jew/Gentile distinction as "in the flesh by human hands." The new dwelling is "in the Spirit" (v. 22; NRSV: "spiritually"), a temple that has not been made by humans (v. 21). Verse 12 reminds the audience that they were once "without Christ." Now they are built on the cornerstone that is Jesus Christ (v. 20). Finally, verse 12 speaks of Gentiles as being alienated from the polity of Israel, as strangers and "without God in the world." Now they can count themselves as fellow citizens and members of God's household (v. 19).

Phrases from Col 1:19-22 inform Eph 2:14-16. Colossians describes "peace" as the reconciliation with God brought about through Christ's death on the cross. However, Colossians does not provide the image of a dividing wall of hostility that is central to Ephesians (vv. 14, 16c). Ephesians departs from the cosmological perspective of Colossians, which referred to reconciling heaven and earth, to focus on soteriology, which has brought Jew and Gentile together in a single body.

◊ ◊ ◊ ◊

11-13: "Remember" (vv. 11-12) calls the audience's attention back to their former state just as "you were dead" did at the beginning of verse 1. They were once called "the uncircumcision" by the "circumcision." What is the significance of such an observation? The description of circumcision as "in the flesh by human hands" downplays its crucial significance as a sign of the covenant with God (Gen 17:11-14). Echoes of earlier Pauline conflicts seem to be at work (Gal 2:1-14; Phil 3:2-3; Col 2:11). The fact that Jews required circumcision was well known (Josephus *Ant.* 1 §192; Tacitus *Histories* 5.5,2).

Colossians 2:11 speaks of believers receiving a circumcision "not of human hands" (see 2:13). Within first-century Judaism, references to "spiritual circumcision" or circumcision of the heart distinguish members of sects that claim true devotion to God from other Jews (Deut 10:16; Jer 4:4; *Jub.* 1.23; Philo *Spec. Leg.* 1.305; 1QpHab 11:13; 1QS 5:5). By speaking of the "circumcision made in the flesh by human hands" (also Rom 2:25-29), the speaker in Ephesians dissociates himself from those Jews who used the derogatory term "uncircumcised" for the Gentiles. The expression "in the flesh" was used for those born Gentiles in verse 11a (NRSV: "by birth") and then for the external circumcision of Jews in verse 11b. Whatever exists merely "in the flesh" cannot express God's new creation (v. 10).

Lest the audience shrug off this bit of ethnic backbiting, verse 12 details the privileges enjoyed by those who belong to Israel. The formulation echoes Rom 9:4-5, but has converted positive statements in Romans to negative expressions describing what the Gentiles lack. The list begins where Rom 9:4-5 ends, with Christ. Romans 9:5 treats the fact that the Christ [= messiah] was Jewish as the culmination of Israel's privileges. The opening "without Christ" in Eph 2:12 forms a counterpart to the beginning of verse 13, "but now in Christ Jesus" and stands in parallel to the concluding phrase "without God in the world."

The middle two phrases of verse 12 situate the deficiencies—being without the Christ, hope, and God—in the fact that the audience did not belong to the Jewish people. Ordinarily the term "alienated" (NRSV: "being aliens") refers to separation from someone or something to which one was formerly attached. This meaning hardly fits the case of Gentiles and Israel, since the Gentiles were excluded from the prior covenant (Exod 19:6; Pss 80:8-9; 105). The term "commonwealth" (or "body politic") can be used of those who possess citizenship rights. Ephesians may be referring to the Old Testament depiction of Israel as God's people (Deut 5:1-3; Isa 65:9) rather than the particular ethnic or citizenship status of Jews and Gentiles. The phrase "covenants of promise" serves as a generalizing reference to the Old Testament covenants.

The emphasis on uniting Jew and Gentile suggests a context that includes actual experiences of Jew and Gentile separation in the first century CE. Jewish exclusiveness frequently led to charges of misanthropy (Josephus *C. Apion* 2 §258; Tacitus *Histories* 5.5.1). There is considerable debate over the extent to which first-century Jews encouraged sympathetic Gentiles to join the commonwealth of Israel (see Goodmann 1994). When the initiative came from the Gentile convert, Jews did accept proselytes (*C. Apion* 2 §210). Relationships between Jews and Gentiles in the cities of Asia Minor seem to have been more complex than a simple division suggests. For example, inscriptions and other documents show that Jews and Gentiles exchanged benefactions (Trebilco 1991).

Evidence for relationships between followers of Jesus and the Jewish communities of Asia Minor remains scant (Sanders 1993). Paul's sufferings there (2 Cor 1:8-9) appear to have been at the hands of civil authorities. Matthew's polemic against the Pharisees reflects the situation in Syria (Matt 23:34-36). Expulsion of Johannine believers from the synagogue cannot be securely located (John 9:22). The "synagogue of Satan" sayings in Revelation do refer to cities in Asia Minor (Rev 2:9; 3:9). Josephus preserves evidence from the first century BCE that Jews in Asia Minor asked Roman authorities or local city councils to confirm their rights to follow ancestral customs (*Ant.* 14 §259-61; 16 §163; see Feldman 1993). By the beginning of the second century CE, there are fledgling Christian churches in all the cities of Asia Minor where we know of Jewish communities. This convergence suggests that these Christian groups began among the Jews of the synagogues (Feldman 1993, 73).

The description of what Gentiles lack may have been common in Jewish communities. The related expression in Col 1:21 lacks the details about belonging to the community of Israel and sharing its covenant promises. The expression "without God" in Eph 2:12 refers to a frequent motif in the Bible, that is, the Gentiles are ignorant of God (LXX Jer 10:25; 1 Thess 1:9; 4:5; Gal 4:8). The expression can be used for someone considered to be godless in the sense of impious. That usage makes it parallel to the expression "those who are disobedient" in verse 2 (so Gnilka 1980). In that case, the meaning of Eph 2:12 would be close to Gal 4:8, "not know[ing] God . . . enslaved to beings that by nature are not gods." However, the expression "without God" might reflect local polemics. Josephus reports the slander against Jews that they were "atheists (*atheoi;* "without God") and haters of humankind" (*C. Apion* 2 §148).

Despite the Jewish cast to its depiction of Gentiles, the "now" does not speak of Gentiles joining the commonwealth of Israel. Instead, Ephesians uses the expression "brought near by the blood of Christ" (v. 13). Ephesians 1:7 spoke of redemption in Christ's blood as forgiveness. More immediately, readers have been reminded that they are exalted in the heavenly places with Christ (2:6). This set of spatial terms would lead the audience to conclude that they have been brought near to God rather than to the commonwealth of Israel as such.

The Old Testament refers to Gentiles as "far off" (see Deut 28:49; 29:22; 1 Kgs 8:41; Isa 5:26; Jer 5:15). The term "come near" or "approach" also appears in Essene writings for joining the sect (1QS 9:15-16) or for the knowledge of the Law, which comes through God's spirit. Persons who "approach" in this sense are separated from others who disregard the Law: "to the degree that I approach my fervour against all those who act wickedly . . . increases; for everyone who approaches you, does not defy your orders" (1QH 14 [= 6]:13-15). Thus for the Essenes, to "come near" could mean increasing distance from other Jews whose observance of the Law did not meet the standards of the sect.

14-18: Attempts to isolate a continuous hymnic piece in verses 14-16 have resulted in very different solutions, though most agree that the phrases "dividing wall" and "in his flesh" (v. 14), "the law with its commandments and ordinances," and "in himself" (v. 15), and "through the cross" (v. 16), are likely to be expansions by the author of Ephesians. Rudolf Schnackenburg prefers to read verses 14-16 as an elaborate periodic sentence similar to those found earlier in Ephesians. Its phrases alternate between references to the negative things that must be destroyed and to the positive result of Christ's coming, making peace. References to Christ are threaded throughout: (a) himself . . . in his own flesh (v. 14); (b) in himself (v. 15); (c) in one body . . . in himself (v. 16).

The negative phrases all refer to what must be destroyed: (a) a barrier (v. 14*b*); (b) Law of commandments and decrees (v. 15*a*); (c) enmity (vv. 14*c*, 16*b*). Unity is not merely the end to human enmity. It also involves reconciliation with God through the cross. Verse 16 is the only explicit reference to "the cross" in Ephesians. This reference is connected with images in this section taken from Col 1:20-22, "making peace," God's willingness to "reconcile," the "blood of his cross," and being "estranged." Ephesians has used the hymnic phrases from Colossians to depict the new unity of Jew and Gentile (Schnackenburg 1991).

Verse 14 shifts from the "you" form of the previous verse to "we." "Christ is our . . ." formulae appear elsewhere in the Pauline Epistles, with Christ being called wisdom, righteousness, sanctification, redemption (1 Cor 1:30); life (Col 3:4); and hope (1 Tim 1:2). Making peace between estranged parties does not always imply that they become "one." The body metaphor requires harmonious concord, but such peace could embrace differentiated parts. However, readers know that God planned to bring all things together in Christ (1:10). If the Gentile deficiencies result from being separated from Israel, one might have thought Ephesians would argue that "brought near" meant incorporation into Israel. Since that is not what occurs, some interpreters assume that Ephesians has the reconciliation of Gentile and Jewish believers in mind (as Rom 15:7-13; Bouttier 1991).

Spacial and socio-political estrangement become enmity in verse 14c. Evidence for severe or sustained hostility between Jews and Gentiles in Asia Minor is weak. If we look to the Essene usage of "come near" for joining the sect, enmity would imply intrasectarian polemic. The pious Essene becomes the enemy of all Jews who are not observant. Ephesians appears to view the Law as a source of enmity, since Christ has made peace by abolishing its various precepts (v. 14b).

Jews often faced the accusation that their Law made them "haters of humanity." Josephus replies that any fair observer would find that the Law has quite a different result. His account of the Jewish constitution should show any reader of goodwill that "we possess laws best designed to produce piety, fellowship with one another and sympathy toward humanity at large, as well as justice, strength in hardships and contempt for death" (C. Apion 2 §146).

The Law as a "dividing wall" that protects the holiness of the people appears in an apologetic context in the *Letter of Aristeas*: "the legislator . . . being endowed by God for the knowledge of universal truths, surrounded us with unbroken palisades and iron walls to prevent our mixing with any of the other peoples . . . thus being kept pure in body and soul . . . and worshipping the only God omnipotent over creation" (*Arist.* 139). The overloaded Greek phrase in Eph 2:14b, *to mesotoichon tou phragmou* ("the dividing wall of the hedge" [or "fence," encircling a vineyard]) may be a reflection of a phrase like the "palisades and walls" of *Aristeas*. (The NRSV translation simply omits the problematic genitive phrase.) By itself, *to mesotoichon* might suggest the dividing wall in the temple area that prohibited Gentiles from entering on pain of death (Acts 21:27-31). The parallel phrase in verse 15a makes it clear that what the author has in mind as the barrier between Jew and Gentile is the Law with its various ordinances.

The sectarian polemic in Essene legal texts connects building a "wall," that is, sectarian legal interpretation, and separation. Echoing Mic 7:1, the *Damascus Document* has "the wall is built, the boundary far removed" (CD 4:12). The same text also speaks of those who have removed the boundary, "builders of the wall" who go astray after false teaching (CD 4:19), "in the age of devastation of the land there arose those who shifted the boundary and made Israel stray" (CD 5:20). Such apostate "builders of the wall," and those who follow their interpretations of the Law, will be subject to God's wrath (CD-B 19:31-32). Concluding a letter that contains a number of Halakic rules concerning temple offerings and purity regulations, the Essene author comments, "we have segregated ourselves from the rest of the people and we avoid . . . associating with them in these things" (4QMMTa 92-93). Since the letter is addressed to an outsider whose group its author encourages to adopt similar Halakic rulings (4QMMTa 113-14), one must assume that such action would lead to reconciliation between the two groups. From a sectarian point of view, destroying the "dividing wall" could only mean destroying the separation created by divergent legal rulings.

The expression *ton nomon tōn entolōn en dogmasin* ("the law of commands in decrees"; NRSV: "the law with its commandments and ordinances") has sometimes been understood to imply that only part of the Law is abolished, the ceremonial or other statutes that divide Jews from Gentiles, or those elements that are "in decrees" made by those who interpret the Law, what the New Testament elsewhere refers to as "traditions of the elders" (Mark 7:5-8; Matt 23:1-4, 15-24; Barth 1974). The assumption that the Law is divisible has little support in Jewish texts. Both apologetic writers like Josephus and *Aristeas* and intrasectarian texts like the CD and 4QMMT assume that Moses' legislation including the peculiarly Jewish rites and customs and proper Halakic interpretation belong together. As the Essenes would say, interpretation enables individuals to "turn away from the path of the people on account of God's love" (CD-A 19:29). Therefore, Ephesians refers to the whole Law. The additional nouns, "commandments and ordinances," exclude understanding what is abolished as a sectarian reading of the Law.

Though Paul carefully avoids speaking of the Law as "abolished" (Rom 3:31), Ephesians has no concern to affirm the divine character of the Law (cf. Rom 7:12).

Verse 15b fills out the positive hints in verse 14, completing the rhetorical structure of the section by matching the final "making peace" with the earlier "he is our peace." The "made both groups into one" is elaborated as "he might create in himself one new humanity in place of the two." Creation of the new humanity is the result of abolishing the Law. Galatians 3:26-28 links being "in Christ" with abolition of the fundamental categories that divide persons. Paul used the formula to support his contention that righteousness that comes through faith has no place for inheriting God's promises by being under the Law (Gal 3:23-25, 29). Since the expression "no male and female" in the Galatians formula alludes to Gen 1:27, the connection between baptism and "new creation" or restoration of the state of humankind prior to its alienation from God probably belonged to the original formula (so Betz 1979; MacDonald 1987).

A Gnostic reading of Eph 2:14-15 would draw upon speculation about the division of Adam and Eve from their original unity. In this myth the creator god gained control over beings who were spiritually superior to him. For example, Adam tells his son Seth, "And we resembled the great eternal angels, for we were higher than the god who had created us and the powers with him. . . . The god, the ruler of the aeons and the powers, divided us in wrath. Then we became two aeons. And the glory in our hearts left us, along with the first knowledge that breathed within us" (*Apoc. Adam* V 64,14-28). Though some Gnostic texts treat baptism as renewing the androgynous, divine image, *Apoc. Adam* concludes with what appears to be polemic against the angelic guardians of baptism for permitting its waters to be defiled (84,5-22). Any who would receive those rites become subject to the rule of the powers.

Unlike either Galatians or later Gnostic readers, Ephesians does not connect its new humanity with baptism. Some commentators spontaneously assume that all conversion language in Ephesians has a baptismal *Sitz im Leben* (Schnackenburg 1991). The expression "new creation" or "new creature" rather than "new humanity" appears in Paul's writings (Gal 6:15; 2 Cor 5:17). Ephesians is probably dependent upon Col 3:10 for the idea. However, Ephesians departs from both Colossians and the later Gnostics by not speaking of the image of God when referring to new creation.

The connection between "new creation" and a humanity reconciled with God through the death of Christ appears in 2 Cor 5:17-21. The connection between verse 15 and reconciliation in verse 16 suggests that Ephesians has that imagery in view (Lincoln 1990). Verse 16 employs traditional formulae about the effectiveness of the death of Christ (see v. 13; Rom 5:10; 2 Cor 5:18). The traditional formulation might have used "body" as a reference to Christ's body. Since Ephesians uses "one Body" for the unity created in Christ, described earlier as exalted head of the Body (1:23), the expression here must refer to the new entity of Jew and Gentile, the church. "Through the cross" indicates that the death of Christ is understood as the sacrifice that brings reconciliation (also 5:2).

Although Ephesians does not use a citation formula, verse 17 alludes to Isa 57:19 (and possibly Isa 52:7) in which the peace is preached *(euangelizein)* to both those near and far off. Verse 18 employs a Pauline theme: all Christians have access to God in the Spirit (Gal 3:18; Rom 5:1-2). The following points of verse 18 parallel verse 16: (a) reconcile to God; access to the Father; (b) both groups; (c) in one Body; in one Spirit; (d) through the cross; through him. It is impossible to tell whether "in" designates the spirit as locus of access to God or as its instrument (Fee 1994, opts for the locative sense). The phrase "in one Spirit" is framed by "access to the Father." It recalls the earlier description of the Gentiles as "without God in the world" (v. 12). The term "access" also brings the audience back to the eulogy in which God was depicted as a powerful benefactor. In a secular context the verb "to gain access" might be used of persons who are fortunate enough to be admitted to the presence of the emperor. Whether ambassadors or individuals, the purpose of such an audience was to press a request for benefits. Readers in the cities of Asia Minor would be familiar with efforts to gain access to the governor as he made his rounds of the province. Verse 18 makes a striking point about abolishing hostility in Christ: access for one group does not mean exclusion for others.

19-22: The next shift in imagery (vv. 19-22) can be linked to the imperial example in verse 18. Access to a powerful person often implied entry into an impressive building. Slaves who served powerful men could assert authority over freedmen of higher status by granting or denying physical access to their master and his household. Cities in Asia Minor vied with one another to secure imperial favor by building a temple to Augustus (Faust 1993). In religious contexts the issue becomes access to God associated with a temple. Ephesians combines both images by calling Christians "members of the household of God" and "holy temple in the Lord." Referring to concrete examples of temple construction, Ephesians depicts the temple as one in the process of being built up (vv. 21-22).

Verse 19*a* returns to the description of the Gentiles as strangers. The term "aliens" refers to persons who dwell in a place that is not their homeland. Since the LXX does not make a sharp distinction between the Greek words translated "strangers" and "aliens," the second may be a rhetorical variant of "stranger." It corresponds to "aliens from the commonwealth of Israel" (Eph 2:12) since aliens do not enjoy citizen rights. First Peter 2:11 uses "aliens" when speaking of Christians in an exhortation to watch their conduct among "Gentiles" [= non-Christians]. The designation "citizens with" reverses their prior exclusion from citizenship. However, the phrase "with the saints" is ambiguous. If verse 19 were strictly parallel with verse 12, "the saints" should be used as in Jewish texts to refer to the righteous of Israel. Since Ephesians has announced the destruction of the Law, it would make little sense to declare that Christ has made the Gentiles "fellow citizens" with Israel. Without its founding legislation, Israel could not claim to be a "commonwealth." Therefore "saints" must designate those who are Christian believers regardless of their origins. The shift from the civic metaphor to the familial, "members of the household" (cf. Gal 6:10), has been prepared by the earlier indication that Christians were preordained to be God's children (1:5).

Verse 20 shifts from household members to the building itself. Paul used a building image in 1 Cor 3:9-11. There the foundation is the Lord, the apostle the master builder, and others build upon his work. Ephesians has shifted the imagery. Christ is portrayed as either a capstone or cornerstone (see below). Apostles and prophets are the foundation. This comment places "apostles" in the past relative to the Epistle and its audience. Ephesians 3:5 explains how the apostles serve as foundation, and how they are the ones to whom the mystery of God's plan has been revealed. The Essene writings show a similar regard for their founder: God's revelation to him provided the insight necessary to found the new community. Since Ephesians uses "prophets" after the term "apostles," it appears to have Christian prophets in mind (for example Matt 7:15; 1 Cor 12:10, 28).

Old Testament texts about the cornerstone in Zion were applied to Jesus (Isa 8:14; Luke 2:34; Rom 9:32; 1 Pet 2:8). However, the capstone held the building together. Its location at the top of an arch also fits Ephesians' consistent references to the exaltation of Christ (4:16). The unity of the initially separate "you" and "us" gains the organic form of a building whose diverse materials must be properly fitted together and held in place by the capstone.

Designation of the building as "temple" retrieves the access to God image from verse 18 along with its reference to the Spirit. Though the phrase "grow" has been seen as discordant with Christ as capstone of a building, it anticipates the later description of the body growing together in the unity of the Spirit (4:3, 11-16). The presence of God's Spirit in the community described as temple was well-established in Paul's writings (1 Cor 3:16; 6:19-20). By shifting to the temple in which the Spirit dwells, Ephesians suggests that the community will be the locus of God's presence in the world (Fee 1994).

◊ ◊ ◊ ◊

Every comment about Jew and Gentile in this section belongs to well-established motifs in Jewish apologetic or sectarian writings except the extraordinary claim that God abolished the Law in order to unify the two. This concern extends Paul's own polemic against those who thought Christians ought to be incorporated into Israel by adopting peculiarly Jewish observances. However, attempts to find a particular Jewish or Jewish Christian problem behind this section of Ephesians have failed. Although verse 12 might suggest that the Gentiles are to be brought into Israel, Ephesians avoids claiming that the church has replaced Israel. In the present reality of the church as a single community built up together in Christ, there is no distinction between Christian and Jew. Even the concern for harmony between Jewish and Gentile believers evident in Rom 15:1-13 is moderated. Nothing in Ephesians suggests tensions between the two groups were creating difficulties (contrast Rom 14:1-23).

It is also impossible to use Ephesians to support theories of an ongoing covenant with Israel that will bring it to salvation outside of Christ. Ephesians consistently insists that God's plan from the beginning has been a "new creation" that requires abandoning the barriers that distinguished Jew from Gentile (see the extended argument in Lincoln 1987). At the same time, Ephesians does not presume that all of the covenants, images, and promises of Israel belong to Gentile Christians by virtue of their Jewish heritage. The church is not separated from the God revealed in the story of Israel, but only exists through God's new act of creation. To recognize Christ's exaltation as head of the body of Christian believers requires an insight into the mystery of God's plan that is not available to nonbelievers.

Indeed, Ephesians leaves no opening for the continuing observance of the Law by Jewish Christians (Sanders 1993). Despite the differences in their origins, both Jewish and Gentile believers are reconciled to God through Christ. Both are brought into the body of Christ and have the same Spirit. They have a common foundation and belong to a building designed to be held together by one capstone. While diversity of origins is no barrier to coming into the church, it is not an excuse for a building of clashing architectural styles! Thus the emphasis on unity in Ephesians rejects the possibility of God's people being divided into multiple sects.

Since all legal ordinances are abolished, the church cannot be a sect within Judaism like the Essenes—a group grounded on claims not only to the spirit, but also to a founder with inspired insight into God's will, and to identification as "the holy ones" of God's promise. Though Ephesians shares many religious images with Essene writings, it does not understand the church as a religious group centered on interpreting the teachings and Halakic ordinances of a human founder. Instead, Ephesians insists that the reality of the church is in its head, the exalted Christ made present through the Spirit. Whatever the particular arrangements in local communities, they should reflect the symbolic truth about the church. Its unity is based in incorporation of different groups into a new humanity that no longer preserves the socio-religious boundaries established by the Law.

Prisoner for the Gospel (3:1-13)

Paul now becomes "prisoner for Christ," a phrase used in Phlm 1. Verses 2-13 read as a long digression until the prayer report introduced in verse 14. The pattern of alternating pronouns continues: "you" (vv. 2-6); "I" to "we" (vv. 7-12); and "you" (v. 13).

Verse 1 is an anacoluthon (an abrupt mid-sentence shift to a different grammatical construction), which identifies the subject but lacks a verb. Verse 2 begins with a "for surely" that assumes that the audience has heard of the mission entrusted to Paul. Verses 3-7 spell out the origins and content of Paul's service. Verse 13 finally states the consequence that is to follow from recognizing what Paul's ministry is: do not be discouraged by his imprisonment (cf. Phil 1:12-13; 2:17-18). The intervening sentences (vv. 8-12) expand the account of Paul's ministry by describing the content of the mystery being revealed. Reference to his boldness (v. 12) anticipates the exhortation to the audience in verse 13, so that they do not "lose heart over my sufferings."

This section forms a key piece of evidence for the hypothesis that Ephesians has drawn on the text of Colossians. It combines the sequence of topics in Col 1:23-28 with echoes of earlier parts of Ephesians, especially the previous section (2:11-22). Table 1 sets out the parallels between the two letters; a more literal translation has been provided to make the verbal parallels clearer.

Table 1: Eph 3:1-13 and Col 1:23-28

Theme	Ephesians	Colossians
Introduce Apostle	[3:1] I Paul the prisoner for you	[1:23c] I Paul a servant (Eph 3:7)
		[1:24a] . . . for you
Sufferings of the Apostle	[3:1] prisoner [3:13] in my trials for you	[1:24b] the deficiency of the trials of Christ in my flesh for his body
Office of the Apostle	[3:7] of which I have become a servant	[1:25] of which I have become a servant
	[3:2] the administration of the grace of God given to me for you	[1:25] according to the administration of God given to me for you
Revelation of the Mystery	[3:4-5a] the mystery of Christ that was not known to other generations	[1:26] the mystery that was hidden from the aeons and the generations
	[3:9] the mystery hidden from the aeons	
	[3:5] has now been revealed to his holy apostles and prophets	[1:26] but now has been manifested to his holy ones
Content of the Mystery	[3:6] that the Gentiles would be an inheritance with, body with, and sharers with the promise in Christ Jesus through the gospel	[1:27] the wealth of the glory . . . in the Gentiles, which is Christ in you, the hope of glory
Mystery Preached	[3:8] to preach to the Gentiles the	[1:27-28a] to make known what the wealth

	incomprehensible wealth of Christ	of the glory of this mystery in the Gentiles, which is Christ in you . . . whom we announce
God's Power in the Apostle	[**3:7c**] according to the activity of his power	[**1:29b**] according to the activity that is working in me in power

Ephesians has taken the basic structure of Paul's self-presentation from Colossians. In verse 3, "as I wrote" suggests that the audience would be familiar with the existence of other Pauline Epistles. References to Eph 2:11-22 demonstrate how carefully this section has been integrated into the Epistle: (a) you Gentiles (v. 1; 2:11); (b) "holy apostles and prophets" (v. 5; 2:20); (c) "with" expressions to designate incorporation of Gentiles (v. 6; 2:19); (d) share a promise (v. 6; excluded from promise, 2:12); (e) in body of Christ (v. 6; 2:16); (f) access to God (v. 12; 2:18). Other expressions point to earlier sections of Ephesians: (a) "commission" (Gk. *oikonomia*, "administration"; vv. 2, 9; 1:10); (b) grace of God (vv. 2, 7, 8; 1:6, 7; 2:5, 7, 8); (c) mystery revealed (vv. 3, 4, 9; 1:9); (d) rulers and powers (v. 10; 1:21); (e) heavenly places (v. 10; 1:3, 20; 2:6).

Rhetorically, the account of Paul's ministry serves to establish the character of the speaker. Such descriptions often appear as digressions in ancient rhetoric. A key requirement is establishing the reliability of the speaker. Since the audience has no personal knowledge of Paul on which to judge his character, Ephesians asserts that they can discern the truth of his claim to special insight from what he has written (vv. 3-4). Ephesians also establishes a relationship between the apostle and his audience by reminding them that the apostle's suffering benefits the Gentiles (from Col 1:24-25; also see Phil 1:5-7). The exhortation not to lose heart over his sufferings (v. 13) adds an element of pathos to the relationship between Paul and the audience.

◊ ◊ ◊ ◊

1: "This is the reason" (v. 1) connects this section with the previous reference to the Gentiles being incorporated into the temple of God (2:22-23). The addition of "for the sake of you Gentiles" integrates the biographical notice into the theme of bringing Gentiles into the body of Christ. Verse 13 does not spell out how suffering is integral to the apostle's mission. Readers may be familiar with Paul's view that suffering confirms the connection between the apostle and the crucified (1 Cor 4:1-13; 2 Cor 6:3-11). Just as the cross is not a major theme in Ephesians, so apostolic hardships are not a topic of discussion. The letter contains only two other references to the sufferings of the apostle (v. 13; 6:20). Both connect his imprisonment with bold speech. Neither passage uses the reference as evidence for the heroism of the apostle (contrast 2 Tim 2:8-10; *pace* Martin 1991, who equates Ephesians and 2 Timothy). Nor does Ephesians develop the soteriological picture of apostolic suffering in Col 1:24 (*pace* Bouttier 1991).

2-7: The first half (vv. 2-4) of the lengthy digression in verses 2-7 recalls what the audience may already know about Paul. Description of Paul's mission as "commission" (Gk. *oikonomia*) is taken from Col 1:25. Ephesians also uses *oikonomia* as God's plan of salvation (1:10; 3:9; NRSV: "plan"). In those cases, "plan" connects the saving activity of God with the order established in creation. Consequently, the "commission" entrusted to Paul is part of the process by which God's plan to unite all things in Christ is effected. The experience of God's grace involves understanding the divine purpose in Christ (1:9-10).

Paul used the phrase "stewards *(oikonomoi)* of God's mysteries" in 1 Cor 4:1. There the expression "mystery" reminds readers of the cross as the mystery unknown to the powers (1 Cor 2:7). For Ephesians, "mystery" refers to bringing together all things in the exalted Christ. Verse 3 attributes the apostle's knowledge of the mystery to revelation.

The Essenes also attributed the insight of their founder to divine revelation. Revelation to the elect is essential to their salvation (1QS 11.6-7, 15-19). We have seen that Ephesians does not treat its revelation as the key to a sectarian version of inherited Jewish tradition. Nor does Ephesians argue that Paul's preaching represents what was already revealed in scripture (contrast Gal 3:6-22; 4:21-31; Rom 4:1-25).

The phrase "as I wrote before briefly" (AT; "as I wrote above in a few words" NRSV) is enigmatic. In ordinary correspondence, it would imply previous communication between the author and recipients. Or in some instances it would refer to attached correspondence (see White 1986, nos. 4 and 7). However, Ephesians is not a letter between parties who have business or friendship with each other. Although its author is familiar with Paul's letters, and particularly Colossians, a reference to "wrote briefly" hardly suggests a collection of Paul's epistles. The NRSV translation ("as I wrote above in a few words") follows exegetes who conclude that the expression refers to an earlier passage in Ephesians (1:9-10; 2:11-22). But Ephesians could be assuming prior reading of individual Pauline letters or extracts from them in the churches (Meade 1986). Verse 4 makes the reading of the letter, itself, evidence of the apostle's insight.

In describing that mystery (vv. 5-7), the Epistle returns to motifs already presented, especially in 2:11-22. The "with" verbs in verse 6 pick up use of such expressions in 2:19-22. The foundation stone of the building to which the Gentiles are joined in 2:20, the "apostles and prophets," are now the privileged recipients of insight into the mystery of Christ.

By insisting that the mystery was unknown in past ages, Ephesians appears to assert that not even the righteous persons or prophets of the Old Testament had knowledge of the blessings to come to the Gentiles (Lincoln 1987). However, the phrase should not be pressed to yield a theology of prior revelation. In apocalyptic writings such revelation formulae indicate that readers now have insight into divine mysteries that have been concealed from the rest of humanity (e.g., Matt 13:17). In a historical apocalypse, the seer receives both a vision and its interpretation. Since the vision refers to future events, only divine inspiration could provide the required understanding (Dan 10:1). Or the apocalypse may reveal hidden wisdom given to an ancient seer but sealed until the time of fulfillment (Dan 12:9; 2 Esdr 14:5-10). Thus "not made known . . .

now revealed" is a way of indicating that the time of fulfillment has come. The reference to "apostles and prophets" (v. 5; 2:20) indicates that the author of Ephesians does not consider Paul the sole recipient of insight into God's plan of salvation.

The expression "*his* holy apostles and prophets" supports the claim that Ephesians was not composed by Paul. He would have used the expression "us apostles" (as in 1 Cor 4:9). Verse 7 uses the self-designation "servant of the gospel" from Col 1:23. Paul uses the Greek term *diakonos* ("servant") in a variety of senses: (a) political rulers, who need not be aware of a place in God's order (Rom 13:4); (b) individuals in local churches (Rom 16:1; Phil 1:1); and (c) himself [and Apollos] as missionaries who established churches (1 Cor 3:5-7; 2 Cor 3:6; 6:4). Since the false teachers who had come to Corinth take on a false appearance as "servants (NRSV: "ministers") of righteousness" (2 Cor 11:15), "servant" plus a genitive expression was probably a common term for traveling missionaries.

Ephesians takes over the depiction of God's power from Col 1:29. However, it drops the reference to apostleship as weakness and struggle found in Col 1:29*a*. Stylistically Ephesians needs a shorter phrase. Thematically, the sufferings of the apostle are not the topic of discussion. Ephesians repeatedly stresses the extraordinary manifestation of God's gracious power in the salvation of the Gentiles. (See the use of "power" in 1:19. The power of God demonstrated in the resurrection and exaltation of Christ may have been taken from Col 2:12, so Barth and Blanke 1994.)

8-13: Ephesians breaks off the previous sentence only to begin describing the apostle's mission again (v. 8; contrary to the NRSV, v. 7 belongs to the digression that began in v. 2). The passage opens with a striking description of the apostle as "least of all the saints." Readers familiar with Paul's letters immediately think of his self-designation, "least of the apostles" (1 Cor 15:9). The apostle uses his late call and efforts in founding churches as evidence for the power of God's grace working in his mission (1 Cor 15:10). Since Ephesians has consistently used "saints" for believers, referring to Paul as "least of all the saints" is somewhat puzzling. Earlier

Ephesians described the Gentiles as being added to the "saints" [= "us"], fellow "citizens with the saints" (2:19). The apostle whose knowledge of the mystery of God makes this incorporation possible can hardly be described as "least" among Christians. The expression may be dictated by the rhetorical requirements of self-praise. By having Paul deprecate his own achievement, Ephesians has him magnify the graciousness of the divine benefactor who has given him the task of preaching the gospel (Schnackenburg 1991).

The summary of his message intensifies earlier formulations of the mystery embedded in God's creative plan. The Greek text of verse 9a is uncertain. The twenty-seventh edition of the Nestle-Aland Greek text brackets the "all" (NRSV: "everyone") following the infinitive "to enlighten" (NRSV: "to make see"). The problem is finding the referent of "all" (Gk. *pantas*). It does not agree grammatically with "Gentiles" in verse 8. "Saints" is too far away from the adjective, and such an assertion would in any case contradict the expression "least of the saints." Therefore some interpreters prefer to follow the manuscript tradition that lacks *pantas* (NRSV note: "to bring to light"). On that reading, the apostle illuminates the mystery, itself, not individuals about the mystery (so Schnackenburg 1991).

However, Eph 1:18 asks God to enlighten the addressees. To "enlighten the heart" occurs in apocalyptic language as God's activity. Paul claims such enlightenment for his preaching in 2 Cor 4:6 with reference to God's creation of light in Gen 1:3. The "I" of the Essene teacher is described as mediating the divine illumination he received from God to the community through his teaching, "like perfect dawn you have revealed yourself to me with your light" (1QH 12[= 4]:6); "you exhibit your power in me and reveal yourself in me with your strength to enlighten them" (1QH 12:23); "through me you have enlightened the face of the Many . . . for you have shown me your wondrous mysteries" (1QH 12:27). Comparison with Essene language indicates that "all" stands in place of its designation for those illuminated through the Teacher, "the many." Despite the grammatical difficulties, it would have to refer back to "the saints." The NRSV translation "make everyone see" does not capture the appropriate nuances of transmitting what is essentially

God's illumination of the hearts of the elect. It suggests that the apostle fulfills a routine teaching task to provide cognitive information about God's design.

As the Essene example indicates, divine illumination operates within the community of those chosen by God. Readers of Ephesians know that community is the church. The cosmic images that Ephesians uses for the church also have some roots in this type of apocalyptic terminology. The church identifies with the exalted Christ, just as the Essenes spoke of their sect as joining the heavenly community of the "holy ones" [= angels], "He [= God] unites their assembly to the sons of the heavens" (1QS 11:8). From that perspective, it is not difficult to see how Ephesians can conclude that the church, which belongs in the heavenly regions with Christ, would make God's hidden plan of salvation apparent to the various powers of the universe (vv. 10-11). As we have already seen, the terminology of divine predestination "in accordance with the eternal purpose" belongs to this revelation pattern (v. 11; 1:11). Therefore, there is no reason to treat the "aeons" and "powers" in verse 10 (NRSV: "rulers and authorities") as mythological, hostile powers actively seeking to prevent souls from reaching heavenly regions as in Gnostic accounts of salvation (*pace* Schlier 1957). Ephesians does recognize the existence of evil forces in the cosmos that are defeated by God (2:2; 6:12). The existence of the church serves as evidence of God's power over evil. The teaching of individuals in the church is not a contest against mythological powers (*pace* Conzelmann 1985; see Lincoln 1990).

Nevertheless, scholars continue to link the cosmological terms in Ephesians with religious cults that personified the soul's ascent into the heavens as a defeat for planetary powers. The claim that its author was opposed to the cosmic speculation in the Mithras cult (Cargal 1994) depends upon reading "aeons" as a reference to the god Aion rather than as a temporal term designating "ages." Readers familiar with the zodiacal grades and astronomical speculation attached to the Mithras initiation rites could understand Ephesians to mean that such mystery cults have no power to liberate the soul. However, the apocalyptic terminology used throughout the letter suggests that the temporal reading of "aion" is intended in Eph 3:9-11.

Verse 12 returns to the apostle's character. Boldness in speech was widely regarded as an attribute of the wise or of those, like Moses, favored with special access to God. Both meanings are evident in Ephesians. Paul's boldness is demonstrated in apostolic preaching despite imprisonment (6:19-20). He does not teach for human rewards or he would speak in a way that flatters the audience (1 Thess 2:2; 2 Cor 3:12; Phil 1:20; Philo *Spec. Leg.* 1.321). In the religious context, "boldness" belongs with access to God in prayer, a motif already mentioned in 2:18 (Job 27:10; Philo *Heres* 5-7; Josephus *Ant.* 2 §4.4; 5 §1.3). Both uses connect with what follows. Bold speech in defense of the gospel belongs to the image of the imprisoned apostle (v. 13); direct access to God in prayer, to the prayer formula of verses 14-21.

The final sentence in this section returns to the personal relationship between the author and addressees that opened the long digression (vv. 1-2). Although their only connection with the apostle is through reading, the audience should have such appreciation for Paul's role in bringing salvation to the Gentiles that they despair at his suffering. Ephesians leaves the connection between Paul's suffering and the "glory" that accrues to the Gentiles undefined. "Glory" is always associated with praising God or God's gift of salvation in Ephesians (1:6, 12, 14, 17, 18; 3:16, 21).

Accustomed to the catalogues of apostolic suffering in other Pauline letters, the dramatic pictures of Paul in prison and on trial in Acts, and later martyrdom stories, readers might expect to hear about the imprisoned apostle in Ephesians. Commentators often bring in details from 2 Timothy in referring to this section of Ephesians as the portrayal of a heroic martyr. Yet Ephesians has less to say about the apostle's sufferings than any other Pauline letter. The reference to bold speech and the willingness to suffer for such speech serve as proof of character. They indicate that the message has not been crafted to flatter or suit the prejudices of an audience and that the speaker does not seek some personal gain or advantage.

This section of Ephesians concerns the message that God entrusted to the apostle, not the personal details of his life.

The description of the mystery of God in verses 5-11 follows the same pattern of rhetorical celebration evident in the earlier sections of Ephesians. Its claims are repeated using established patterns of language for divine revelation, election, and salvation. Throughout this section of Ephesians the activity of God's gracious power forms the basis for many statements about human activity. Neither the apostle as one who brings enlightenment about the divine mystery, nor the church as manifestation of the many-sided divine wisdom (v. 10) possess what they convey. Depiction of the church as heavenly reality, not as a human institution, should not be taken as triumphalism since its truth is a mystery of God's plan known to the elect, not an expansionist socio-political program.

From that perspective, Ephesians considers the church as the culmination of God's plan for the entire universe. Therefore, anyone who does not respond to the gospel and become one with Christ has no hope of salvation. Ephesians does mean to say that God intends all peoples to become one in Christ. It presents the church as the new humanity that results. But it is also important to note the perspective from which Ephesians makes such claims—a position of socio-political powerlessness. Christian communities emerged at the margins of Jewish communities, which were themselves minorities in the urban centers of Asia Minor.

The dramatic opening, "I Paul am a prisoner for Christ," evokes the fragile character of the early Christian movement. Its Jewish heritage, especially the apocalyptic images of divine election, provided an extraordinary self-understanding as the church was being transformed from a sect of Jewish believers into a Gentile church of Jewish heritage. Ephesians reminds readers of two essential factors in this surprising development: the sure grasp of God's mysterious plan by particular individuals (especially Paul), and the power of God working to extend salvation to all.

The Apostle's Prayer (3:14-21)

"For this reason" picks up 3:1. The section continues with a prayer report (vv. 14-19) and concluding doxology (vv. 20-21). The petitions (vv. 16-19) ask that the process of salvation be completed in the hearts and minds of the letter's recipients. The doxology returns to the theme of God's power at work within the community of faith.

This prayer report exemplifies boldness and access to God (v. 12). Since the apostle entrusted with the "commission of God's grace" (v. 2) prays for them, readers can be certain that God will grant his request. There is no reason to treat the petitions as evidence of difficulties in the churches (*pace* Lincoln 1990). Because the prayer asks for the love of Christ and fullness of God (v. 19), it forms an appropriate rhetorical conclusion to the speech in praise of God's powerful grace (Fee 1994). The letter next turns to a different type of speech, ethical exhortation (4:1–6:20). That section of the letter is framed by references to Paul's imprisonment (4:1; 6:20). The prayer report facilitates the transition between the two halves of the Epistle by disposing the audience to a Christian way of life.

The prayer report reintroduces the theme of love. The addressees are known for love (1:15). God's love for us (2:4) has been demonstrated in the election to holiness, "to be holy and blameless before him in love" (1:4). The prayer report speaks of the community with its *roots* and *foundation* in love (3:17), an echo of the earlier image of the church in which Gentiles *grow together* with Jews into the temple *founded on* apostles and prophets (2:20-21).

◊ ◊ ◊ ◊

14-15: The apostle's kneeling position (vv. 14-15) departs from the usual custom of standing to pray (as in Mark 11:25; Luke 18:11, 13). Luke has Jesus kneel in Gethsemane (Luke 22:41) rather than lie prostrate on the ground as in Mark (Mark 14:35). Luke also refers to kneeling at prayer in Acts (Acts 7:60; 9:40; 20:36; 21:5). With the exception of Acts 9:40, all of these scenes are associated with death. Jesus and Stephen are about to die. Paul is departing on the journey to Jerusalem that will lead to his imprisonment and death. Kneeling is often the gesture of suppliants begging for a favor from a powerful or important person (as in Mark 1:40; 10:17; Matt 17:14). In these scenes, kneeling expresses the deep emotions of those involved; here it adds pathos to the image of the imprisoned apostle.

The prayer includes a play on words that cannot be easily reproduced in English. He prays to the Father *(patēr)* from whom every *patria* ("clan," "group derived from a single ancestor," "race") is named (the NRSV translation "family" must be understood as a reference to the extended family). Ephesians follows the common Christian tradition of referring to God as "father" ("and the Lord Jesus," 5:20, also 6:23; "our Father," 1:3, also 2:18, 4:6; "of Jesus," 1:4; "Father of glory," 1:17 AT). But what is meant by the assertion that every clan "in heaven and on earth" is named from the Father? Some interpreters suggest that the phrase implies that God is superior to all the powers because he created them. Persons tempted to use the names of heavenly powers for magical purposes fail to recognize the origin of all those names in God (Arnold 1989; Cargal 1994). Others suggest some form of hellenistic cosmological speculation (Bouttier 1991). Stoic cosmology proposed a biological image of the origins of all things out of the divine spiritual substance, "God, mind, fate and Zeus are all one, and many other names are applied to him. In the beginning all by himself he turned the entire substance through air into water" (Long and Sedley 1987, 46B). God appears as father in Platonist cosmologies as well (Plato *Tim.* 28C; 37C; 41A; Philo *Spec. Leg.* 2.165; 3.189). In Gnostic cosmologies, the "first" Father generates all of the subsequent aeons of the heavenly pleroma (e.g., *Ap. John* II 2,27-5,11).

Though Ephesians uses images characteristic of the cosmology of its time, the letter shows no evidence of debate on the subject. Its emphasis on God as creator (also 4:6) provides the general context for this play on words. Everything belongs to the one clan because everything has been created by the one Father-creator.

16-19: The first petition (vv. 16-17) returns to God's power (1:17-23). It also contains variations of phrases from Colossians ("riches of glory," 1:27; "hearts held together in love," 2:2; and "rooted and built up in him," 2:7). Two parallel expressions ask for inner strengthening of the faithful. The first depicts God as the agent of inner strengthening (v. 16). The power through which God raised Christ operates through believers (1:19; 3:6). Unlike Rom 7:22, Ephesians does not use the expression "inner being" (NRSV: "inmost self") as the antithesis to outer, bodily passions that overwhelm reason. Nor does the expression refer to the "new humanity" (NRSV: "new self") of 4:24 (*pace* Schlier 1957). The parallel phrase in verse 17, "in your hearts," indicates that "inner being" refers to the basic intelligence and will of human persons.

The second formulation of the petition (v. 17) specifies what is meant by the first. Strengthening by God's Spirit is not a prior condition for the indwelling of Christ. The phrase "rooted and grounded" is a variation on the "rooted and built up" of Col 2:7. Since it also designates God's mercy and goodness toward the elect (v. 19; 2:4), "love" means both God's love in the faithful and their love for others (1:15).

The second petition (vv. 18-19a) indicates the other fruits of the Spirit. It also consists of two parallel expressions: understanding and knowing are the objects of stengthening (1:9, 17; 3:4-5). The first object of understanding is not clearly specified. "Breadth and length and height and depth" (v. 18) are not dimensions of a particular object. The cosmological images in Ephesians might lead one to anticipate that they refer to God's presence to all parts of the cosmos (as in Ps 139:7-12). Only God's wisdom can comprehend the cosmos (Job 11:7-9). Sirach 1:1-10 personifies God's incomprehensible wisdom. At the same time, she is a gift that the Lord bestows on the righteous: "It is he who created her; he saw her and took her measure; he poured her out upon all his works, upon all the living according to his gift; he lavished her upon those who love him" (vv. 9-10). Ephesians 3:10 presented God's multisided wisdom as manifest to the powers through the church. These petitions ask that God endow believers with the wisdom needed to hold fast to the gift of salvation.

Others suggest that the expression indicates expansion of the human mind or spirit. An apocalyptic reading would treat "the saints" as a reference to the angelic hosts. The object whose dimensions are comprehended would be a heavenly object such as the new Jerusalem (Rev 3:18; 21:6; Ezek 48:16-17) or the temple of God (Ezek 40:1–43:12). An extremely fragmentary wisdom text from Qumran that is introduced as instructions from a sage to the righteous contained a section involving something with roots from the heavens to the abyss being measured by God (4Q298). In another fragment, astronomical measurements had special significance as the hidden wisdom conveyed in a vision of the heavens ordered from God's throne by the movements of the sun and moon (4Q286 Frag. 1). Members of the sect needed this knowledge in order to follow a liturgical calendar that is in accord with the divine order. Participation in divine wisdom is also a presupposition of these texts. Although the apocalyptic timetable is foreign to Ephesians, Essene language is not. Exaltation to the heavens where Christ is seated on the divine throne would certainly endow the saints with such knowledge. It also sets them among the angels. Since Ephesians is using figurative language, not discursive description, a Jewish liturgical fragment may have been the basis for this prayer formula.

More distant possibilities include philosophical reflection on the ability of the human mind to encompass the vast expanses of the cosmos. In interpreting Exod 33:23, Philo distinguishes the mind's ability to know all things that exist below God from its inability to grasp the divine, "it is an ample gift for the best sort of mortals, knowledge of things bodily and immaterial below the Existent" (*Nom.* 8-9). He also repeats an argument for natural knowledge of God as creator based on a survey of the order and harmony of the universe from the region of fixed stars down to the earth (*Leg.* 3.99). Such knowledge is contrasted with direct apprehension of God apart from created things given to Moses (*Leg.* 3.100-101). Though Ephesians might concur with views, nothing in the letter suggests a philosophical interest in the modes of knowing God.

Since "fullness" occurs in the final petition (v. 19*b*), the dimensions of the heavenly pleroma in Gnostic speculation have also been seen as the referent of this phrase in verse 18*b*. Only those whose origins lie in the heavenly church can conceive the dimensions and properties of the aeons that have come forth from the Father (so *Tri. Trac.* 58, 29-60,1). Reading Ephesians as a response to magical practices leads to comparison with prayers and spells designed to gain divine power for individuals (Arnold 1989). The four dimensions are named in a prayer that the magician is to say in order to draw down and retain divine light (*PGM* IV 970-85; Betz 1986, 57).

The parallel expression in verse 19*a* indicates that Ephesians is not concerned with knowledge in terms of human minds stretched to their limits in apprehending the creator or with cosmological speculation but with the experience of the love of Christ (cf. Rom 8:38-39). Ephesians characteristically uses "the exceeding" (Gk. *to hyperballon*) with expressions for salvation ("immeasurable greatness of his power," 1:19; "immeasurable riches of his grace," 2:7). The shift from knowledge to "faith and love" in verse 17 indicates that Ephesians is not a speculative tract. There is no polemic in Ephesians against knowledge (unlike Col 2:2-3). The strengthening to which the prayer refers points to earlier images of the community, not to individual knowledge of God or the cosmos.

The final petition (v. 19*b*) reinforces this orientation. The community must become what the church in its heavenly reality already is, "filled with all the fullness of God." The phrase echoes Colossians, which speaks of the "fullness of deity in Christ" (see Col 1:19; 2:9) and of believers "filled in him" (see Col 2:10). Ephesians 1:23 has already established the immediate context for this phrase. The church is the "fullness of Christ" who in turn fills the entire cosmos. The expression "fullness of God" in this petition highlights the theocentric element in the Epistle. God's preordained plan that culminates in Christ is the object of praise. The shift to divine fullness also indicates that no future revelations or acts in the drama of salvation remain to be achieved (Lincoln 1990).

20-21: The concluding doxology (vv. 20-21) cannot be entirely divided from the earlier prayer, since this is the only doxology in the New Testament to mention Christ and the church as the locus of praise. The reference to both "all the saints" and Christ in verses 18-19 makes this focus appropriate. The doxology also fits the pattern of alternating pronouns so evident in the Epistle. The "you" of the earlier prayer formula is once again joined to the author's "we." In addition, the reflection on God's power working within the believing community picks up both the reference to being strengthened in power (v. 16) and to being filled with God (v. 19). Therefore the doxology should be seen to flow from the intercessory prayer formula (Fee 1994).

Doxologies refer to the person being praised, contain a praise formula—usually with the word *glory,* an eternity formula, and often a concluding amen. The doxology typically occurs at or near the end of a letter ("to our God and Father be glory forever and ever. Amen" [Phil 4:20]; also 2 Tim 4:18; Heb 13:21; 1 Pet 5:11; Rom 16:25-27). The doxology in Rom 11:36 concludes the theological section of that letter as is the case here. Though doxologies are not ordinarily attached to a previous intercession, Phil 4:19 belongs to an expression of thanks that comes close to a prayer formula. The gifts that the Philippians have sent Paul in prison are to be repaid by Paul's "master God." Paul assures readers that their gift is a pleasing sacrifice (Phil 4:18) and that "God will repay (NRSV: "fully satisfy") every need of yours according to his riches in glory in Christ." Many of the terms in this sentence (fill, wealth, glory, in Christ) appear in Eph 3:14-19.

Ephesians begins by celebrating the power of God to deliver even more than humans might ask or think. It retrieves the description of the great power of God that raised Jesus and is at work in believers from 1:19-20. The doxology also models the praise of God's glory for which the elect were predestined (1:6, 12).

◊ ◊ ◊ ◊

This ringing affirmation of God's extraordinary power picks up a note that is already evident in the intercessory prayer report: believers have received the grace and Spirit of God long before they come to ask God for them. Such confidence is part of the access to God that Christians enjoy. The extraordinary character of such expressions becomes evident when one considers the normal mode of making a request of a powerful person or benefactor. Not only should the request be enveloped in extensive praise of the patron's goodness, it is also hedged with, "if it would not be too much trouble . . . ," "if you could . . . ," and other similar expressions. If the person from whom one seeks a favor is considerably more powerful, intermediaries or a prior note of introduction will be produced. It is possible to see all of Ephesians 1–3 as an exposition of God's saving power. The intercessory prayer report and doxology merely confirm what the letter has already stated. God has gathered the elect into the heavenly regions with Christ. In Ephesians, the apostle does not intercede with God to do things. Instead, the prayer asks God to bring to perfection the work of salvation that has already begun among the elect. What that will mean in the concrete terms of Christian life remains to be spelled out in the second half of the Epistle.

Ethical Exhortations on Living as Christians (4:1–6:9)

Building the Body of Christ (4:1-16)

Ephesians presumes that conversion leads to moral renewal. The new moral life is indicated by the self-designation "saints" [= "holy ones"], praise for mutual love (1:15), indications that the elect are "holy and blameless" (1:4) before God, and created for good works (2:10). Paul's letters frequently include sections of parenesis (from Greek *parainesis:* moral advice or admonition). Pauline parenesis has stronger ties to the forms and content of hellenistic philosophers than other sections of his epistles (Malherbe 1992). Ancient moralists held that people should be reminded of what they know so that they will act accordingly (Dio Chrysostom *Orations* 17,2). Therefore the Epistle's parenesis need not reflect actual vices among the addressees. These moralists also held that a teacher's life was to provide a visible example of his teaching.

This section returns to the image of the imprisoned apostle (4:1) and establishes friendship between author and audience that was also considered fundamental to hortatory discourse. Paul's parenesis often opens with the verb *parakalō,* "I beg" (or "I appeal"; Rom 12:1; 2 Cor 10:1; 1 Thess 4:1), and a brief list of virtues (v. 2). The beginning then shifts from convention to a theme of the letter: unity in the body of Christ (vv. 3-6). Verses 2-4 draw on Col 3:12-15. Verse 7 makes the transition from exhortation to the heavenly exaltation of Christ (vv. 8-10). His status is the basis for the gifts of salvation. The conclusion (vv. 11-16) describes unity as working together in the body of Christ. This concern refers back to the growth image (2:21).

◊ ◊ ◊ ◊

1-6: The exhortation to "lead a life worthy of [your] calling" echoes Jewish understanding of divine election. God's calling is to create a people who are devoted to God's law. God works, "to enlighten the heart of man, straighten out in front of him all the paths of justice and truth, establish in his heart respect for the precepts of God; it is a spirit of meekness, of patience, generous compassion, eternal goodness . . . potent wisdom which trusts in all the deeds of God and depends upon his abundant mercy . . . of generous compassion with all the sons of truth" (1QS 4:2-5). Though Pauline churches no longer follow the Law, the conviction that election leads to a new life remains (1 Thess 2:12).

An exhortation to holiness could be expanded by a list of virtues (Eph 4:2-3). For the Essenes, the virtues distinguish the community of the "sons of light" from the "sons of darkness," whose vices that text goes on to describe (1QS 4:9-11). The list in Eph 4:2 "humility, gentleness, patience" adopts the final three of the list in Col 3:12. These virtues are found in the Essene example also. "Humility" does not appear outside Jewish and Christian lists. To the non-Jew, "humility" suggests demeaning lowliness (Spicq 1994). "Gentleness," on the other hand, does have positive connotations in hellenistic ethics. It is opposed to wrath, disposed to forgiveness and to moderate punishment, and lives without jealousy or spite (Aristotle *N.E.* 4.11, 1125[b]; Plato *Republic* 3.387). Those who have this trait can bear hardship or loss with tranquillity. "Patience" also belongs to both traditions. In Jewish and Christian sources it appears as an attribute of God (Jer 15:15; Rom 2:4; 9:22; 1 Tim 1:16; 1 Pet 3:20) or of human beings (Prov 25:15; Gal 5:22; 2 Cor 6:6).

The exhortation "bearing with one another in love" appears in Col 3:13 and in the Essene description of the "sons of light." "Love" can be the foundation of all Christian virtues (1 Cor 13; Gal 5:14).

Galatians 5:15 uses negative examples to highlight the communal implications of the love command. It dictates how persons relate to, and speak about, one another.

Verse 3 shifts to the specific focus of this section: unity. Two clauses, "unity of the Spirit" and "in the bond of peace," indicate that the fruit of the Spirit is peace (Gal 5:22; Rom 8:6; 14:17; 15:13). "Peace" as gift of the Spirit goes beyond social interest in communal concord. It refers to the fullness of salvation that comes from God (Rom 14:17; 15:13). The term "bond" derives from Col 3:14-15 in which love is described as the "bond of perfection" (NRSV: "love, which binds everything together in perfect harmony"). It also creates a verbal echo with the apostle's self-designation "prisoner."

The reference to election from Col 3:15 introduces a list of "one" expressions (vv. 4-6). It ends with the one God who governs and fills the entire cosmos (v. 6). Some interpreters treat verses 4-6 as an independent liturgical fragment (Barth 1974). However, the section appears to be an ad hoc creation from standard Pauline expressions. First Corinthians 12:12-13 (one body, Christ, one Spirit, baptized into one body) provides an initial framework for verses 4-5, while 1 Cor 8:6 provides a formula for God's creative activity. Gordon Fee proposes an essentially trinitarian structure in the series that he calls "one of the more certain and specific Trinitarian passages in the corpus" (Fee 1994, 702). The first term in each verse provides its key image: one body (v. 4), one Lord (v. 5), and one God (v. 6). The first two verses indicate how persons have become part of the body that is God's elect. Verse 6 has taken over a philosophical formulation for the creative activity of God (cf. Pseudo-Aristotle *On the Origin of the World* 6.397b, 11.14-15; *Cher.* 125-26).

Conversion included coming to know the one God, creator of all (Eph 2:12*b*, 18). The creation formula that indicates the transcendence of God, God's activity, and God's omnipresence undergirds the letter's insistence that other forces in the cosmos have no effective power.

7-10: Verse 7 incorporates exhortation by referring to "grace." The expression "each of us was given grace" resembles Rom 12:6, where diversity of gifts is associated with the particular grace given to each person in the community. Ephesians substitutes "according to the measure of Christ's gift" for "grace given." This usage conflates Rom 12:6 with the reference to "measure" in Rom 12:3. There Paul warns against false estimation of one's own gifts. If Ephesians has this section of Romans in view, then one would anticipate what follows in verses 11-13, a discussion of gifts that require proper understanding of one's place in the community.

A digression interrupts the development that verse 7 anticipates. Ephesians has depicted the creative activity of God as equivalent to the plan that culminates in the Body of Christ (1:9-10, 20-23; 2:5-7; 3:9-11). Verses 8-10 contain another description of the soteriological activity of Christ. It uses a form of biblical exegesis familiar from the Qumran scrolls, the *pesher* (see Dimant 1992). Citation of a section of biblical text is followed by its application, often introduced by the formula, "its interpretation is that . . ." (e.g., Isa 40:3 in 1QS 8:13-16; Isa 24:17 in CD 4:13-15). Interpretation involves demonstrating that the biblical text refers to events connected with the past, present, or future [= end of all things] history of the sect. 1QpHab 7:4-5 treats the pesherim as revelations of divine mysteries, "its interpretation (Hab 2:2) concerns the Teacher of Righteousness, to whom God has disclosed all the mysteries of the words of his servants, the prophets."

Ephesians 4:8-10 is a pesher on Ps 68:19 (67:19 LXX). Fragments of a pesher on this psalm have been found at Qumran (1QpPs = 1Q16). That commentary connects with Ps 68:12-13, 26-27, 30-31, but the remains are too slight to permit any reconstruction of the sect's understanding. Ephesians may have taken its citation from a comparable text.

This type of interpretation begins with the theme and continues with as many details as fit the subject. Subunits of a text may be picked up, cited with an introduction, "as for when it says," and followed by additional identifications. Applied to Eph 4:8-10, one sees that the only phrase from the psalm citation on which the pesher comments is "he ascended." Nothing is said about either the "captivity taken captive" or the gifts bestowed on humankind. It is easy to link both of these themes to the overall imagery of Ephesians by understanding "captivity" as the powers to whom Christ's ascent reveals God's plan. The author has "he gave" found in the psalm in both verse 7 and verse 11. But the connection is not made in the exegetical style of a pesher. Therefore the psalm interpretation was not originally formulated to fit the parenesis in verses 7 and 11-16.

Taken as a fragment of early Christian exegesis, the opening argument of the pesher is strikingly similar to John 3:13, "no one has ascended into heaven except the one who descended from heaven, the Son of Man" (also Bouttier 1991, who makes too much of the Moses typology). A related piece of exegesis is connected with the use of Ps 110:1 in Acts 2:32-35 as David's prediction that the risen Jesus would be exalted to God's right hand. That psalm was incorporated into Eph 1:20-23. The argument in Acts 2:34 seeks to show that David was speaking prophetically of the Christ and not of himself. All of these examples use the ascent and descent imagery to advance Christian claims for Jesus as the one who has been exalted to God's right hand.

Both the form and content of the pesher suggest that the regions to which Christ descends refer to the earth, not to some region below the earth (unlike Rom 10:7; 1 Pet 3:18-21; Rev 1:18). The objection that "lower regions of the earth" cannot mean simply earth and must mean Hades ignores the fact that the regions of the air are also connected with earth in ancient cosmology (so Cargal 1994). Since Ephesians does not interpret the phrase about captives, one cannot treat it as the key to the passage as Arnold does in proposing that Eph 4:9 refers to initiation rites that involved descent to Hades (Arnold 1989). The NRSV provides a suitably ambiguous translation, "the lower parts of the earth." Though Eph 2:2 distinguishes the heavenly regions from the "air" (the area below the moon that has malevolent powers responsible for evil), it never refers to regions below the earth (contrast Phil 2:11; Schnackenburg 1991).

The final clause, "that he might fill all things" (v. 10), fits the cosmological perspective of Ephesians. The phrase "filling the universe" was used earlier in connection with God's power and with the exalted Christ in his Body (1:23; 3:19). Ephesians 4:13 speaks of the Christian community maturing in the "full stature of Christ." Cosmological images always serve the soteriological framework of the Epistle. Here, the omnipresence of God (Eph 4:6; as in Philo *Leg. All.* 3.4; *Vita Mos.* 2.238) grounds the image of Christ as universal savior. God's preordained plan only becomes known when Christ is exalted in the heavens.

11-16: Verse 11 picks up the gifts mentioned in verse 7. A single Greek sentence (vv. 11-16) links a list of teaching functions in the community (vv. 11-12) with the need for the church to grow to perfection (vv. 13-16). Romans 12:3-8 orders those gifts that might cause division in the community: prophecy, ministry, teaching, exhorting, contributing to charity (NRSV: "the giver"; for this meaning of the verb, cf. Job 31:17; Prov 11:26; Luke 3:11), serving as a leader (Gk. *proistamenos,* "standing at the head"; with this meaning, cf. 1 Thess 5:12; 1 Tim 5:17; Josephus *Ant.* 8 §12.3 sec. 300; Fitzmyer 1993), and performing acts of mercy (NRSV: "the compassionate"). Romans associates each task with a requisite virtue. These virtues provide the "measure" by which the performance of members of the community can be evaluated.

Ephesians 4:11-12 begins with a list of such functions, but unlike Rom 12:7-8, the list extends beyond the local church. "Apostle, prophet, evangelist" are clearly external to local churches. Ephesians has twice used "apostles and prophets" in a way that suggests an activity that has already been completed (2:20; 3:5). The term "evangelist" only appears in two other places in the New Testament (Acts 21:8 [Philip]; 2 Tim 4:5 [Timothy]). In both cases, the evangelist has been commissioned by the apostles to preach the gospel. Though the term "pastor" appears to be a particular designation for Peter (John 21:15-17), 1 Pet 5:1-5 indicates that the term applied to those who served as elders in the local communities of Asia Minor (also Acts 20:28). A pre-Christian example that uses the term "shepherd" for the community's supervisor also appears in an Essene text (CD 13:7-11). Teachers appear in all the Pauline lists of church offices (Rom 12:7; 1 Cor 12:28). Teaching may refer to basic instruction or to ongoing exhortation (Gal 6:6). Paul can refer to himself as "teacher" (1 Cor 4:17; Col 1:28; 3:16), though "teacher" comes third after apostles and prophets in 1 Cor 12:28. Thus Ephesians begins with those functions connected with the founding of the community and moves on to those of local leaders (Schnackenburg 1991).

Ephesians treats these activities as service to the body of Christ (as in 1 Cor 12:12, 27-30; Rom 12:4-8). Diverse manifestations of the Spirit in the community are forms of service (so 1 Cor 12:5). Verses 12b-16 describe the purpose of service as equipping and building up the body. Paul used the verb "build up" in arguing that love should govern relationships among members of the church (1 Cor 8:1; 10:23; 14:3-5). Ephesians 2:21 used the noun "structure" for the church as a temple being built for the Lord. That building is also spoken as "growing," an image that this section will connect with both "body" and "love" in verse 16.

Although the particular offices refer to those who are in charge of guiding churches after the apostle's death, Ephesians assumes that all Christians are part of the building process (cf. Gal 6:1-6). Maturity involves the community as a whole, not merely particular individuals. A series of short phrases describes the goal of ministry: unity of faith, knowledge of the Son of God, "perfect man" (NRSV: "maturity"), measure of the full stature of Christ (v. 13). All of these phrases appear to be equivalent to the "new humanity" created in Christ (Eph 2:15). That expression described unity in concrete terms, Jews and Gentiles joined in a single community. But if the Jewish believer gives up those elements of the Law that make him or her Jewish, then the "Jewish" side of the equation loses its significance (Sanders 1993). Ephesians 4:4-5 included with "one Spirit, one Lord, one God," the terms "one body, one faith" and "one baptism." Presumably the "unity of faith" and "knowledge" depicted as future goals in verse 13 represent the same faith and knowledge that Christians already experience.

If the "unity of knowledge" is both present experience and future goal, then Ephesians is not dependent upon Gnostic images of the church as a heavenly aeon. For Gnostics, the gathering of the scattered light from the world of darkness into the heavenly pleroma could be said to complete the deficiency in the heavenly church (e.g., *Tri. Trac.* 23, 3-23).

The contrast between maturity and childishness (vv. 14-16) is commonplace in ethical exhortation. Paul uses it to castigate the Corinthians for their divisions (1 Cor 3:1-4). Philo uses "tossed around on the sea" for idolaters whose souls lack the necessary anchor in knowledge of the true God (*Decal.* 67). The problem of "trickery" and "deceitful scheming" that can lead the elect astray adds elements from Jewish apocalyptic to the philosophical picture of those who are morally immature. Essenes had to be on guard against the spirit of deceit (1QS 3:21-22). Early Christians also anticipated the emergence of false prophets within their communities. The expression "deceit" for false teachers appears in later writings of the New Testament (Jude 11; 1 John 4:6; 2 Pet 2:18; 3:17; also Acts 20:29-30; 1 Tim 4:1; 2 Tim 3:13). Since the author of Ephesians has read Colossians, he knows that Paul had warned against specific forms of false teaching (Col 2:2-4, 8). Since the word *scheming* appears in 6:11 for the devil (NRSV: "wiles"), the phrase "deceitful scheming" may suggest a demonic source for false teaching.

The concluding phrases in this long sentence shift back to the positive conditions for building up the Body of Christ, speech as "the truth in love." Paul used "love" as the key to communal solidarity (Rom 12:9-10). Love for fellow members was characteristic of the Essene sect (1QS 1:9). Since Ephesians refers to "speaking truth in love" in contrast to deceit, its concern appears to be speech rather than solidarity. Jealousy and divisive speech show that the Corinthians remain "people of the flesh, as infants in Christ" (1 Cor 3:1). Paul's open presentation of the gospel contrasts with the cunning of false teachers (2 Cor 4:2; 6:7). Truth opposes the error of false teaching, and love opposes its deceit (Lincoln 1990).

Verse 16 echoes the exhortation in Col 2:19 to resist false teaching. Ephesians shifts its focus from the head holding parts of the Body together to the Body's growth into Christ (as in Eph 1:22-23). All of the parts need to work properly for the body to grow. The verb "knit together" appeared in the architectural image of Eph 2:21. The phrase "every ligament . . . as each part is working properly" draws on terms used earlier in the letter: "according to the power (*energeia*; 1:19-20; 3:7) in measure (*metron*; 4:7, 13) of each part." Though Ephesians has specified the functions of other parts of the Body, the term "measure" implies God's gift to each one. Ephesians also uses *energeia* ("power") for God's active power present in the exalted Christ and working through the apostle. Though Ephesians does not make such associations, some interpreters assume that the ligaments are the teachers and "each part" the other members. Consequently, Rudolf Schnackenburg concludes that Ephesians seeks to strengthen the power of the teachers in the community. Their office binds others to Christ.

◊ ◊ ◊ ◊

Parenesis played an important role in early Christian churches. Both teachers and individuals were expected to engage in such hortatory speech. Concern for the unity of religious and civic communities was also a common topic of deliberative rhetoric. Unlike the use of the "body" metaphor in 1 Corinthians and Romans, Ephesians does not point to a crisis of disunity. Exhortation serves the function of reminding the audience of what has already been true of its experience. Election requires that Christians live a style of life appropriate to that calling. Most of the concrete virtues listed (vv. 2, 14-15) support social cohesion, since they moderate competitive, divisive behavior.

The formula "one faith, one Lord, one baptism, one God" underscores the dilemma of religious pluralism. The phrases indicate that for Ephesians there can only be one true people of God. Those who are not part of the "Body of Christ," whether Jews or Gentiles, are not included in salvation. The generalities of such formulae make a surface unity possible. The problems arise when people ask what the practical consequences ought to be. Ephesians does not grapple with situations of communal discord as Paul does in 1 Corinthians or Rom 14:1–15:13. The comments in verses 11-16 suggest general emphasis on building up the church so that all grow to maturity in faith through sound teaching, speech that reflects love, mutual concern, and support of others. Ephesians does not explain how such activities are parceled out. Who are the shepherds and teachers? How do they relate to those founding figures in the common tradition, the apostles, prophets, and evangelists? How do the gifts that each member of the community receives serve the common task of building up the body of Christ?

The catalogues of charismata in Rom 12:6-8 and 1 Cor 12:8-11 that have influenced this section of Ephesians provide one possibility for filling out the picture of individual activities within the body of Christ. Other interpreters reach back to the earlier section on the unity of Jew and Gentile (2:14-22). The "one" formula refers to bringing those who were formerly divided together in a single community, body, and temple building. Following medical discussions of the time in which the operation of the body was explained by its being articulated and joined together with the head through nerves, Ephesians can attribute all of the growth in the body to Christ. The special feature of this body for Ephesians is bringing into one the foreign peoples to whom the gospel has been preached (Usami 1983).

Two Ways of Life (4:17-32)

The call to turn aside from a past way of life occurs in hellenistic moralists as well as in Christian catechesis. Those who were addressed as "you Gentiles" (2:11) are now encouraged to separate themselves from the immorality of the Gentiles (4:17; cf. 1 Pet 2:12). Rhetorically, this introduction creates a boundary between the readers and the larger world (Lincoln 1990). The section divides into two parts: (a) the vices typical of the outsiders (vv. 17-24), and (b) a catalogue of virtues (vv. 25-32) that characterize the "new self" (v. 24). This division reflects a common theme in parenesis—description of the "two ways," virtue and vice. In Essene writings, the ways of the sons of light (members of the sect) are contrasted with those of the sons of darkness (1QS 4:2-17).

Ephesians continues to use "we" for the author and audience. Address to the audience as "you" returns when the list of injunctions is expanded in verses 29-32. The genre of hortatory discourse (instruction by someone who exemplifies the teaching given) makes the "you" address more appropriate than the inclusive "we." Verses

17-24 establish the two groups, "alienated from the life of God" and "renewed in . . . your minds." Verses 25-32 contain a series of imperatives or moral *sententiae*. Verse 25 is the topic sentence that refers to one negative action, "putting away," and one positive one, "speak truth." Verses 26-31 describe what is to be put away, while verse 32 turns to positive relationships among Christians. This section has close relationships to Rom 1:21, 24 and Col 3:5-10 as Tables 2 and 3 indicate.

Table 2: Eph 4:17-19 and Rom 1:21, 24

Item	Ephesians	Romans
non-Jews lack effective knowledge of God: mind	**4:17c** in emptiness *(mataiotēs)* of their minds	**1:21** they have been given over to worthlessness *(emataiōthēsan)* in their thoughts
non-Jews lack effective knowledge of God: darkened intelligence	**4:18a** being darkened in understanding	**1:21** their foolish heart was darkened
consequences of idolatry: impurity	**4:19** they handed themselves over to the practice of every impurity	**1:24** God handed them over to impurity

Ephesians uses a graphic description of the Gentile way of life to encourage readers to remain separated from their former conduct. Colossians provides images for both the old way of life and the new human beings that Christians have become:

Table 3: Eph 4:17-24 and Col 3:5-10

Item	Ephesians	Colossians
not like the Gentiles	**4:17** you no longer walk as the Gentiles walk	**3:7** in which you also once walked

vices: impurity, greediness	4:19 in practice of every impurity in greediness	3:5 sexual immorality, impurity, passion, evil desire, and greediness (which is idolatry)
put off old human being	4:22a put off from yourselves the old human being according to the former way of life	3:8 now you put off . . . 3:9 having taken off the old human being with the deeds . . .
reject passions of old human being	4:22b corrupted according to the passions of error	See vices in 3:5
renew the intellect	4:23 be renewed in the spirit of your mind	3:10 renewed in knowledge
put on the new human being	4:24 and put on the new human being	3:10 and having put on the new
the new creation	4:24 created according to God	3:10 according to the image of the one who created him

Ephesians has not followed the order in Colossians and has introduced stylistic variants in phrasing. Verses 20-21 are a rhetorical appeal to the audience. They follow an established practice in parenesis, invoking prior instruction. The variations in describing the new creation may have a theological motivation. Since verse 24 ends with a reference to the moral categories of righteousness and holiness, Ephesians is not thinking of the elect as created in God's image but as predestined to a way of life.

The second section (vv. 25-32) continues to echo Col 3:8-12. Both are employing a standard form of ethical teaching—lists of vices to be avoided and virtues to be practiced. This form of teaching is so common in antiquity that the vices in such a list should not be culled for evidence about the community. A number of the items in this section will reappear in what follows: (a) not conducting oneself like the Gentiles (4:25–5:2; 5:3-14, 15-20); (b) darkness (v. 18; 5:8, 11; 6:12); (c) error (v. 18; 5:6); (d) impurity and greed (v. 19; 5:3, 5); and (e) righteousness (v. 24; 5:9; 6:14).

◊ ◊ ◊ ◊

17-24: Ephesians reminds the audience to reject the Gentile way of life (vv. 17-24). The word *Gentiles* was previously used for Christians of Gentile origins in contrast to Jewish Christians (2:11; 3:1). Now it designates "pagans," non-Christian Gentiles. Other phrases suggest baptismal conversion: "testify in the Lord" (v. 17*a*), being "unclothed" (NRSV: "put away") and "clothed" (NRSV: "clothe yourselves") (vv. 22, 24; Bouttier 1991; Schnackenburg 1991). The rest of the sentence uses characteristic terms for Gentile ignorance of God (e.g., Wis 12-15; 18:10-19; *Arist.* 140; 277; *Sib. Or.* 3.220-35). Romans 1:19-21 employs similar language. Having abandoned knowledge of the creator, the Gentiles are locked in immorality and worship of false gods. Ephesians uses two expressions that refer to the mind: "futility of mind" and "darkened understanding." The LXX uses "understanding" interchangeably with "heart." In the Old Testament the "heart" is the seat of the understanding. Ephesians has drawn its terminology from Rom 1:21, "they became futile in their thinking" and "their senseless minds (Gk. "hearts") were darkened." Ephesians has expanded the series to involve two forms of mental darkness followed by "hardness of heart" (v. 18). The Old Testament frequently refers to disobedient Israel as hard hearted (Ps 95:8; Isa 6:10; 63:17; Jer 7:26; 17:23).

These phrases fill out the earlier reference to non-Christians as "those who are disobedient" (2:2). Such language seeks to gain an emotional response, not to provide information. All three descriptions are consequences of being separated from the "life of God" (4:18). This expression does not answer the question of whether or not any trace of God's life remains with those who do not know the creator. Rather, being alienated from the "life of God" describes those who are not participants in the covenant (Eph 2:12). Unfaithful Israelites can also be described with such language as Essene examples indicate, "for futile are all those who do not know the covenant. And all those who scorn his [= God's] word he shall cause to vanish from the world" (1QS 5:19-20).

The concluding clause presents typical examples of pagan vice (v. 19; cf. Rom 1:24). The cover term "impurity" appears in Essene material as the contrary to the holiness that comes from joining the new covenant community (1QS 5:20-21). Unlike Rom 1:24 in which God hands the Gentiles over to immorality, Ephesians makes the Gentiles responsible for handing themselves over to vice. The Greek word that describes their having become callous (apēlgēkotes) only occurs here in the New Testament and is not widely used elsewhere. Ephesians employs a few standard vices as illustrations—disordered sexual passions, greed, and uncleanness. Their only purpose is to awaken revulsion for the life that believers have left behind.

Verses 20-21 repeat the appeal to follow prior instruction with the unusual phrase "learn Christ." For some interpreters the continuation "as truth is in Jesus" suggests an audience familiar with traditions about the teaching of Jesus (so Schnackenburg 1991). Others think Ephesians is combating speculation that separated the heavenly revealer from the earthly Jesus (so Schlier 1957). The text does not explain what is meant by the cryptic expression, though prior catechesis must be implied (Gnilka 1980).

Verses 22-24 are based on Col 3:8-10. They combine two motifs used for conversion: changing clothing (putting off vice, putting on Christ [Rom 13:12, 14; 1 Thess 5:8]) and transformation from the old human being (Rom 6:6) into the new (Gal 3:27; Col 3:10). Putting off vices (see *Arist.* 122; Lucian *Dial. Mort.* 10.8.9) and putting on virtues (see Philo *Conf. Ling.* 31) are commonplace in ethical exhortation. The difficulty with reading the old and new "man" as Adam and Christ (Rom 5:12-21; so Barth 1974) is that Paul always defers the believer's conformity to the image of Christ as spiritual Adam to the future resurrection (1 Cor 15:22-23, 53-54; Phil 3:21).

The general exhortation to "be renewed in the spirit of your minds" (v. 23) indicates the end of the intellectual deficiencies of pagan reasoning. The parenesis in Romans begins with a similar expression ("be transformed by the renewing of your minds," Rom

12:2). Ephesians has radicalized the inherited images by describing the believer as completely re-created "according to God" (see v. 24; Bouttier 1991, Gnilka 1980). Ephesians omits the term "image" from Col 3:10. Most interpreters assume that the Greek "according to God" *(kata theon)* means "according to the likeness of God" (so NRSV). However, Ephesians has shown little interest in the creation speculation of Colossians. The phrase "according to God" is complemented by the virtues that describe God's elect, "righteousness and holiness" (Schnackenburg 1991). It antici-pates the phrase in 5:1, "be imitators of God," and is oriented toward the present behavior of believers (Lincoln 1990). The Essene writings also employ the contrast between "deceit" and "truth" to distinguish those who belong to the community from outsiders (1QS 4:2-5:10).

25-32: Ephesians shifts to a series of short exhortations, *senten-tiae* (vv. 25-32), that describe vices to be avoided and virtues to be cultivated. Colossians 3:8-9, 12-13 provides the core for Eph 4:25-32. Each exhortation describes what is to be done and pro-vides a reason for such conduct. Truthful speech is to replace lying because of the corporate character of Christian life, since all are "members of one another" (v. 25; 4:12, 16; Rom 12:4-5). Ephesians 4:15 treated "speaking the truth in love" as key to building up the body of Christ. The connection between anger and work of the devil (v. 27) echoes Gen 4:7 (and 6:11; Bouttier 1991). The topic of anger occurs in Greco-Roman moralists (Plutarch *On Controlling Anger* 452E-464D), the Sermon on the Mount (Matt 5:21-22), and in Essene writings (see CD 7:2-3). *Testament of Dan* 5:1-2 provides the virtue of truth-telling with a motive clause that includes God's presence to the community and driving Beliar away.

This reference to the reformed thief (v. 28) has no parallel in Colossians but is also traditional (see 1 Cor 6:10; 1 Pet 4:15). The alternative in the second clause, laboring with one's hands, was established by Paul's own example (1 Thess 4:11; 2:9; as part of the apostolic hardship list, see 1 Cor 4:12; against the disorderly who take advantage of communal charity, see 2 Thess 3:6-11). Ephesians has generalized the advice. The motive clause points toward a communal concern, sharing what is gained by such labor with those in need. Exhortations to share appear elsewhere without the reference to earning one's own living (see Rom 12:13; 2 Cor 9:6-12). Such examples might suggest that the apostle merely requires those Christians who are wealthy enough to include fellow Christians among those who receive their benefactions (see 1 Tim 6:17-19).

The need to engage in manual work (v. 28) indicated in the catalogues of Paul's hardships by the phrases "in toil and hardship" (2 Cor 11:27) or "the work of our own hands" (1 Cor 4:12); "working for a living" (1 Cor 9:6); "worked night and day" (1 Thess 2:9) describes the situation of the majority of believers (1 Cor 1:26). They are to provide for themselves and others rather than seek to live off of wealthy patrons (1 Thess 4:11-12; 2 Thess 3:6-13). Some interpreters suggest that the original warning against stealing also spoke to particular social issues (Gnilka 1980). Slaves or other servants were commonly accused of theft (e.g., Phlm 18; Titus 2:10). Thus, this advice ensures the respectable behavior of Christians who are not among the elite and whose affiliation with the new religous movement might render them suspect.

Verse 29 returns to the opening theme. Concern for what one says, here expressed by the Semitism, "come out of your mouths," is commonplace in Wisdom literature (see Prov 10:31-32; 12:17-19; Sir 5:10-14; 18:15-19). The Essenes required their members to control speech. After warnings against angry speech and lying, the Rule of the Community turns to misuse of communal property, retaliation, and then negligent speech (1QS 7:2-11). Penalties are attached to trivial speech and interrupting one's fellows. The context for this speech among the Essenes is a communal assembly for instruction. Ephesians will refer to assemblies for worship later (5:19). The concern for speech aimed at the religious edification of the hearer suggests conversation among fellow believers, not interactions with outsiders.

The reference to the Holy Spirit (v. 30) interrupts the series of concrete examples. Some commentators treat "and do not grieve the Holy Spirit of God" as a motive clause parallel to "do not make room for the devil" (v. 27) and "as God in Christ has forgiven you" (v. 32; Fee 1994). As such, it reinforces the exhortation in verse 29.

The phrase "grieve the Holy Spirit" is unusual, though 1 Thess 5:18 speaks of quenching the Holy Spirit in the context of communal prophecy. Essene texts refer to "defiling" the Holy Spirit that one has received from God (CD 5:11-12). Neglecting the legal and moral precepts of the sect would be the occasion for such defilement. The phrase itself resembles the prophetic word in Isa 63:10, "they rebelled and grieved his holy spirit."

Ephesians indicates that the Spirit was conveyed in a ritual of "sealing." Since Eph 4:5 referred to "one baptism," the rite in question was probably baptism. The final phrase of verse 30, "for the day of redemption," may also be traditional. It introduces a rare note of future salvation into the letter. This passage highlights the effect of the Spirit in the community. Believers are to feel a particular concern for their behavior because it effects the holiness of the community (Schnackenburg 1991).

Another effect of incorporation into the Christian community, forgiveness (v. 32), serves as the final motivating clause in this section. Verse 31 opens with a list of vices that Christians will avoid (bitterness, wrath, anger, wrangling, slander; see Col 3:5, 8). These vices all refer back to anger (v. 26) and the behavior it causes. Concern to rise above anger and its manifestations forms a common element in both Greco-Roman and Jewish exhortation. The section concludes with communal love and harmony, virtues that are the opposite of the divisions caused by anger (v. 32; cf. Col 3:12-13; Gal 5:22). God's forgiveness as the motive for Christian forgiveness appears in Col 3:13 (as well as the Lord's Prayer; see Matt 6:14).

◊ ◊ ◊ ◊

Though composed of shorter exhortations, this section can be seen as the continuation of the last section. That section concluded with the metaphor of the body of Christ joined together and growing to maturity through love (vv. 15-16). The primary focus of both the virtues and vices developed in this section can be said to be communal harmony. The audience must remain committed to a way of life that is unlike their previous life as "pagans," a life that accepted greed, sexual immorality, and other evils. Of course,

Ephesians and its readers know that there were philosopher-preachers who sought to turn humans away from their irrational accommodation to passions that swamp rational human behavior. True to its Jewish heritage, however, Ephesians assumes that those who are ignorant of the true God will not be capable of any consistent moral insight or activity.

Ephesians expresses an understanding of Christian life that runs throughout the Pauline tradition. Christians have been transformed in Christ. The Spirit of God works in the community of believers to effect a new way of life. At the same time, Christians must be actively engaged in strengthening what they already are. Conversion, baptism, putting off the old and putting on the new human being, being sealed with the Spirit and freed from sin are not past events whose effects remain, as though the temple of God were a monumental piece of architecture. Rather, they have introduced believers into a new reality, the body of Christ, which is still in the process of growing into its head. Like the body, the development of the whole depends upon, and contributes to, the well-being of individual members.

The reference to the "day of redemption" reminds the audience that human conduct will be subject to divine judgment. However, the primary emphasis of the Epistle remains the present life of the community. Relations with others are central to the concrete examples of the new Christian way of life. False speech, anger, theft, bitterness, slander, and the like destroy relationships among human beings. The many faces of anger indicate that ethical maturity is fairly rare. Believers would insist that only God's Spirit can transform us from the old way of life to the new.

Ephesians also recognizes that believers must constantly turn away from sinful behavior. They do not claim to be completely free of passions like the Stoic sage. When anger occurs, it must be put away and not harbored (v. 26). Hanging on to anger or other resentments provides opportunity for the devil. As we have seen from the Essene writings, "the devil" actively leads believers away from God. Though it is easy to think that many of the virtues listed in this section of Ephesians are "for saints only," this section does not support such an approach. All Christians are striving toward the holiness and perfection that are given by the Spirit.

The communal emphasis in Ephesians distinguishes its Jewish heritage from treatment of the same themes by pagan moralists. Virtues are not the result of individual reason and its ability to order human life. Rather, God calls together a community of persons to live in holiness and justice. The earlier section of the letter spoke of the Christian community in which Christians—Jewish and Gentile—become one as the new human being (2:15). This creation was also predestined to walk in good works (2:10). The ethical section of the letter depicts those works. Their focus on the needs of others as well as on harmonious relationships indicate how the communal body grows into Christ. Christian community requires face-to-face involvement with others. The forms of speech being recommended are essential to the maturing of the body of Christ, words to support faith, expressions of love and forgiveness.

Live as Children of Light (5:1-14)

References to God and Christ link 5:1-2 with 4:32. A list of vices follows (vv. 3-5). The warning against being deceived contrasts "those who are disobedient" (v. 6) with "children of light" (v. 8). The section ends with a liturgical fragment celebrating Christ as light (v. 14). Some interpreters treat verses 1-2 as the conclusion of the previous section. Others treat all of verses 1-5 as part of the previous section *(UBSGNT)*. They begin a major section with "let no one deceive you" (v. 6) and continue through verse 21. Lists of vices, however, do not typically open sections of parenesis. Therefore 5:1-2 must introduce the list (Gnilka 1980). The *UBSGNT* avoids that difficulty by treating 5:1-5 as the conclusion to a section that begins at 4:25. Their second division picks up the parallelism between verse 6 "let no one deceive you" and verse 15 "be careful then how you live." Since verses 15-21 introduce a new image, the wise and the foolish, we prefer to treat them separately as the transition between the general exhortation and the household code of 5:22–6:9.

Ephesians 5:3-8 draws on Col 3:5-8 as the following chart indicates:

Table 4: Eph 5:3-8 and Col 3:5-8

Item	Ephesians	Colossians
vices not even named among Christians	5:3 sexual immorality and all impurity or greed	3:5 sexual immorality, impurity . . . and greed
vices of speech to be replaced with thanksgiving	5:4 indecency and foolish talk or vulgar talk	3:8 indecent speech
those who have no inheritance in the kingdom	5:5 every evil or impure or greedy person who is an idolater	3:5 and the greed (which is idolatry)
God's judgment falls on the wicked	5:6 for because of these things the wrath of God comes	3:6 through which the wrath of God comes
contrast past with present	5:8 once . . . but now	3:7, 8 once . . . and now

The vices are arranged in groups of three. They pick up themes from the previous section: impurity and greed (4:19), immorality as a consequence of idolatry (4:18), unguarded, degenerate speech (4:29), and divine judgment (4:30).

Ephesians 5:6-14 urges separation from the ways of darkness. These verses echo some of the dualistic language found in the Essene texts and conclude with a liturgical fragment (v. 14) that provides a christological basis for the light imagery (so Lincoln 1990).

◊   ◊   ◊   ◊

1-5: The graciousness of God (4:32) serves as the motivation for an appeal to "be imitators of God" (vv. 1-5). Encouragement to find and imitate a model was a prominent feature of ancient parenesis, "Nay, if you will but recall also your father's principles, you will have from your own house a noble illustration of what I am telling you . . . after whom you should pattern your life . . . regarding his conduct as your law, and striving to imitate and emulate your father's virtue" (Pseudo-Isocrates *Demonicus* 9-11;

in Malherbe 1992, 282). Since the model indicates both what sort of person the young should aspire to be and what they should avoid, advice is typically given in an antithetical form, "not . . . but . . ." (see Malherbe 1992, 283; for Jewish examples see *T. Benj.* 3.1; 4.1).

Paul uses this imitation pattern regularly. Christians may be encouraged to imitate other churches (1 Thess 2:14) or Christ (1 Thess 1:6). However, his most common usage follows the philosophic example of the child imitating a parent. Thus, Paul underlines the "father in Christ"/"child" relationship between himself and those churches he founded (1 Cor 4:14; 11:1; Phil 3:17; 1 Thess 1:6). The "as beloved children" in verse 1*b* recalls this pattern. Christians routinely refer to themselves as children of God (Gal 4:5-6; Rom 5:5; 8:15; Phil 2:15; "destined for adoption," Eph 1:5). However, the injunction to imitate God does not appear elsewhere in the New Testament. Philo does, however, speak of imitating God in the context of those who have power to rule others. They ought to copy God's beneficence, "the best is to use all their energies to assist people and not to injure them; for this is to act in imitation of God, since he also has the power to do either good or evil, but his inclination causes him only to do good. And the creation and arrangement of the world shows this" (*Spec. Leg.* 4.34, 186-87).

Ephesians is not concerned with exercising power over others. Ephesians 4:24 referred to the new human being as "created according to the likeness of God in true righteousness and holiness." This expression develops the motif of the Christian as a new creation in God's image. Therefore, one would expect some account of the virtues that characterize God to follow. The expression "live in love" (v. 2*a*) meets that requirement. God's love was introduced in the opening eulogy as the cause of election to holiness (1:4). "Love toward all the saints" described the audience in the epistolary thanksgiving (1:15; 4:2, 15-16). God's love is expressed in extending salvation to those separated from God by sin (2:4). The Christian's grounding in love is formed by knowledge of the love of Christ (3:17-19). The general exhortation to love in 5:2 continues with an illustrative clause "as Christ loved us" (v. 2*b*). Christ's death as an acceptable self-offering to God provides the concrete example of that love (v. 2c). Ephesians 1:7 uses Christ's death as sin-offering to illustrate the extraordinary graciousness of God in bringing about salvation. The blood of the cross abolished the wall of separation between Jew and Gentile (2:13). This passage uses established formulae to highlight the self-offering in Christ's death (Gal 1:4; 2:20). A more concrete application of the exemplary love of Christ for the community of the faithful occurs when Ephesians applies the image to the traditional motif of the relationship between husbands and wives in 5:25-27.

There is a difference in orientation between the Ephesians vice list (vv. 3-5) and that in Col 3:5-8. Colossians described the vices as being put to death by conversion. In Ephesians, the vice list describes pagan outsiders (4:17). This passage calls Christians to separate themselves from others in their environment. The term "fornication" (Gk. *porneia*) includes a variety of illicit activities including adultery and prostitution (Sir 23:16, 27; Philo *Jos.* 43-44; *T. Reub.* 1.6; 2.1; 3.3; *T. Iss.* 7.2; 1 Thess 4:3; 1 Cor 6:12-20). Fornication and impurity often appear together in vice lists (Gal 5:9; 2 Cor 12:21; Col 3:5; 1QS 4:10). Since the other two sins in the list refer to sexual activities, some scholars suggest that "greed" should be understood as unrestrained sexual greed, such as the violation of the command against coveting the neighbor's wife (*T. Levi* 14.5-6; *T. Jud.* 18.2; 1QS 4:9-10). Ephesians is not merely warning against such behavior (cf. 1 Thess 4:3-8). Rather, Christians are not to even speak of such vices. The conclusion "as is proper among saints" might be trading on the semantic ambiguity of the term "saints." If translated "holy ones," the expression can refer to "the angels." This dual meaning provides the logical force behind the phrase. Such vices would not belong to speech among the angels.

The second triad includes two clear examples of censured speech: foolish talk and vulgar talk. The Greek word *eutrapelia* ("vulgar talk") has a more positive meaning in common usage than it does in this triad. Usually it refers to "witty" or clever speech (Aristotle *N.E.* 4.8, 1128a). The context in Ephesians indicates that the author has one of the Aristotelian excesses in mind: vulgar or obscene speech. This use of the word may reflect a cultural sense that the proper bearing of a wise person requires seriousness in speech.

Persons who are facile with words are less appropriate models than those whose lives exemplify the words they utter: "Let us choose . . . not men who pour forth their words with the greatest glibness, turning out commonplaces . . . but men who teach us by their lives, men who tell us what we ought to do and then prove it by their practice" (Seneca *Epistles* 52,8; Malherbe 1992, 285). Or the term may reflect the sectarian emphasis on disciplined speech that one observes in the Essene documents, "and whoever giggles inanely causing his voice to be heard shall be sentenced" (1QS 7:16). The speech of the Essene sectary avoids all vices, "From my mouth no vulgarity shall be heard or wicked deceptions. . . . I shall remove from my lips worthless words" (1QS 10:21-24).

Prohibited forms of speech are to be replaced by exhortation or thanksgiving. The philosopher exhorts others to virtue. The Essene turns speech to piety and the saving deeds of God: "with hymns shall I open my mouth and my tongue will ever number the just acts of God" (1QS 10:23). The thanksgiving proposed in Eph 5:4*b* fits this pattern. Ephesians 1:3-14 provided a concrete example of the type of speech the author has in mind. Ephesians 5:18-20 returns to the topic of communal speech in prayer and praise of God. Thanksgiving is central to the Christian life and prayer elsewhere in Paul's writings (1 Thess 5:18; Phil 4:6; 2 Cor 4:15).

The conclusion also has parallels in the Essene writings. Though the phrase "kingdom of God" is peculiarly Christian (on exclusion from the Kingdom see 1 Cor 6:9-10; Gal 5:21; 1 Cor 15:50), the "inheritance" terminology belongs to the language of Jewish piety. The wicked do not belong to God's covenant, "all those not numbered in his covenant will be segregated, they and all that belongs to them . . . all those who scorn his word, he shall cause to vanish from the world" (1QS 5:18-19). The righteous receive an inheritance that unites them with the angelic hosts ("sons of the heavens"), "to those whom God has selected he has given them [= righteousness, knowledge of God and so forth] as an everlasting possession; until they inherit them in the lot of the holy ones. He unites their assembly to the sons of the heavens" (1QS 10:7-8).

The vices listed are typical examples of wickedness, sexual immorality, impurity, greed, and idolatry (see Wis 14:12; *T. Jud.* 19.1;

23.1; Philo *Spec. Leg.* 1.23, 25). Paul uses these vices in a longer list of those who *will not inherit* the kingdom (1 Cor 6:9-10). Ephesians employs the present tense "has any inheritance in" instead of the future. The Essene examples show that Jews could speak of both present and future participation in the inheritance of the elect.

The vice triad in verse 5 parallels the list in verse 3 (on the chiastic structure of vv. 3-5, see Porter 1990). The unusual dual genitive in "kingdom of Christ and of God" recalls the references to God and then Christ in verses 1-2. Verse 5 opens with a peculiar phrase, the second person plural of the verb "to know," *iste*, followed by the participle, *ginōskontes*. The form *iste* may be either indicative or imperative. Most translations opt for the imperative and suggest that the additional participle reflects a Semiticizing Hebrew infinitive absolute. Hence the translation "be sure of this" (NRSV). However, some scholars treat the finite verb as an indicative that refers back to verses 3-4, "for this you know." In this case, the participle would refer to what follows in verse 5, and could be translated "recognizing that . . ." (see Porter 1990). This reading makes the general orientation of the parenesis in this section clearer. The author is not correcting believers who lack holiness that they ought to have but is reinforcing an established Christian way of life.

6-14: Ephesians insists on separation between "children of light" and "those who are disobedient" (vv. 6-14). This dualism is characteristic of the Essene writings that have provided parallels for much of the imagery in Ephesians. The Essene texts also show a concern to avoid being deceived. They describe the agent of deceit in mythological terms as the "angel of darkness." The Prince of Lights guides the sectaries, "In the hand of the Prince of Lights is dominion over all the sons of justice; they walk on paths of light. And in the hand of the Angel of Darkness is total dominion over the sons of deceit" (1QS 3:20-22). Ephesians has not mythologized those who may lead its audience astray. There is no evidence that particular false teachers are in view. The unbelieving Gentile world is a sufficient source of "deception" (2:2-3; 4:17-18). Outsiders may seek to counter a Christian's new life by justifying their vices (so

Schnackenburg 1991) or by the sort of ridicule and abuse described in 1 Pet 4:3-5.

The image of the wicked as persons who justify their actions by claiming that God does not judge was common in Jewish writing (see Exod 5:9 [LXX]; Deut 32:47; Wis 2; *T. Naph.* 3.1). In Eph 3:6 the author spoke of salvation as making the Gentile converts "sharers in the promise." Here the same word is translated "be associated with" (v. 7) and warns against sharing in the deeds of those who remain outside Christ (cf. 2 Cor 6:14–7:1). In the Essene case, the call for separation from the "sons of darkness" has a clear sociological meaning. Persons become members of a new community with its own interpretation of the Mosaic Law, ritual calendar, worship, and detailed instructions governing the lives of members. Contacts with outsiders are limited. It would be natural to read Ephesians as requiring a similar withdrawal, except that the letter nowhere hints at the kind of social structures required to sustain such a move. Therefore the dissociation required in this passage seems to apply primarily to the activities that characterized the lifestyle of non-Christians. The emphasis on "fruit of the light" and "pleasing to the Lord" in verses 9-10 suggests that a Christian's general conduct is in view.

Ephesians may also anticipate that Christians will be active moral agents in their world. They are to "try to find out" (Gk. *dokimazontes;* "discern" or "test") what is pleasing to the Lord (v. 10). This expression implies that believers must determine what is suitable behavior in concrete circumstances. For the philosopher, such moral discernment is the activity of reason (Epictetus *Discourses* 1.20,7; 2.23,6). Earlier, Ephesians spoke of the renewal of mind that comes with conversion (4:23). Romans 12:2 treats that renewal as the basis of the ability to discern God's will. Elsewhere Paul also uses the verb *dokimazein* in the sense of taking responsibility before the Lord who is to come in judgment (Phil 1:10-11). Failure to "discern" what is required will lead to divine punishment (1 Cor 11:28-32).

Christian responsibility is not limited to one's own conduct. Verse 11 moves beyond refusal to participate in evil. Christians should also "expose" (Gk. *elenchein*) evil deeds. The verb can refer to divine condemnation (Wis 4:20; 2 Esdr 12:32-33). Or, sinners can be "convicted" by persons who hold up their sin before their eyes (Sir 19:13-17; Lev 19:17 [LXX]; 1 Cor 14:24-25). The philosopher moralist also sought to upbraid hearers for their vices in order to effect reform. The philosopher as a good physician of the soul will vary his speech from stinging rebuke to gentle encouragement as suits the condition of his audience (Dio Chrysostom *Orations* 77/78, 38, 42; Malherbe 1992).

Who is the audience of the rebuke envisaged by Ephesians? Some say it is fellow Christians in danger of falling back into their prior lifestyle (as in Matt 18:15-17; Gal 6:1; so Gnilka 1980). This policy can be found among the Essenes (see 1QS 5:24-25), who have nothing to do with outsiders, "He should not reproach or argue with the men of the pit but instead hide the counsel of the law in the midst of the men of sin. He should reproach with truthful knowledge and with just judgment those who choose the path, each one according to his spirit" (1QS 9:16-18a). Or does Ephesians intend believers to confront outsiders with the evil of their actions? The description that follows in verses 12-13 suggests that the latter interpretation should be preferred. Although the evils that such people do are not to be spoken of among believers (vv. 3, 12), they can be exposed. (See John 3:19-21 for a similar image.) Ephesians does not indicate what form such a confrontation might take. The Epistle presumes that its readers are familiar with the process of conversion in their own experience of moving from darkness to light, from death to life (2:1-2; 4:17-18; Lincoln 1990).

The liturgical fragment that concludes this section (v. 14) clearly marks the transition back to the experience of conversion. The connection between the cryptic phrase "everything that becomes visible is light" and the citation said to illustrate the point is unclear. Ephesians spoke of "eyes of your heart enlightened" to recognize God's offer of salvation (1:18). Essene hymns speak of God "brightening the face" of the righteous or of their teacher: "I give you thanks Lord because you have brightened my face with your covenant. . . . Like perfect dawn you have revealed yourself to me with your light" (1QH 12[= 4]:5-6). This passage contrasts the teacher illuminated by God with deceivers who would lead people astray. The hymnic fragment in Eph 5:14*b* identifies Christ as the source of illumination for the righteous.

The origin of the citation is unclear. Within the Epistle, "death" consistently refers to the preconversion situation. Consequently, the fragment seems to be associated with the baptismal imagery of arising from death (Rom 6:4, 13). The Christian remains awake and vigilant in anticipation of the day of the Lord while others are in darkness or drunken sleep (1 Thess 5:5-8; Rom 13:11-14). Its form is similar to the short fragment in 1 Tim 3:16. Some commentators agree with those patristic authors who saw here images of Jerusalem from Isa 60:1 (also 51:9; 52:1; Bouttier 1991). The Lord has summoned the captive city to awake, be clothed in festal garments, arise and shine because the light of the Lord's glory has dawned. This imagery recurs in descriptions of the coming messiah (*T. Levi* 18.3-4; *T. Jud.* 4.1). Clement of Alexandria in his exhortation to the pagans treats this passage as a word of the Lord (*Protrep.* 9.84).

Other commentators have turned to Gnostic texts that picture humanity lost in drunken sleep until the revealer comes from the divine world of light to awaken them (Schlier 1957). Ephesians was popular among second- and third-century Gnostics. This passage may have inspired the final section of a Gnostic hymn that describes the descents of the revealer: "and I filled my face with the light of the completion of their aeon. And I entered the midst of their prison which is the prison of the body. . . . And I said, 'I am the Pronoia of pure light; . . . Arise and remember that it is you who hearkened, and follow your root, which is I, the merciful one, and guard yourself against the angels of poverty . . . and beware of the deep sleep and the enclosure of the inside of Hades.' And I raised him up and sealed him in the light of the water with the five seals in order that death may not have power over him" (*Ap. John* II 31, 2-25). This Gnostic example also suggests a ritual context that included baptism and sealing against the powers of the lower world. It shares the cosmology of Ephesians in treating salvation as exaltation to a realm above the powers of this world. However, Ephesians does not exhibit the sharp dualism of the Gnostic author. It does not equate the body with the imprisonment of the soul by passions. Nor does Ephesians show characteristic Gnostic tendencies to either ascetic denial of bodily reality or its libertine overcoming. Therefore, Gnostic parallels should be treated as dependent upon Ephesians rather than as its source.

◊ ◊ ◊ ◊

This passage illustrates a feature that characterizes much of the ethical exhortation in the New Testament. On the one hand, lists of fairly specific vices indicate conduct that is unacceptable. On the other, the virtues to be cultivated are phrased in a more general way, such as love or imitation of Christ or discernment of what is pleasing to God. Unlike groups within Judaism—Pharisees or Essenes, for example—Christians did not attempt to specify the positive obligations of Christian life by interpreting the Law. Consequently, they had to constantly ask what conduct pleases God in every particular situation. Hans Dieter Betz has suggested that uneasiness about Christian freedom in the face of human sinfulness led the Judaizers in Galatia to advocate adopting Jewish customs (Betz 1979, 5-8). Ephesians has learned from the apostle Paul that the Law created a separation among people that Christ has abolished.

Because Ephesians is not addressed to a particular crisis, its exhortation only expresses the guiding images of the Christian life. However, this section indicates that Christians take moral renewal seriously. They strive for a perfection that does not even need to speak of the evils that typify life without Christ. This injunction does not imply withdrawing from the world. The exhortation to name evils that are being hidden by others shows that Christians must act as a form of moral conscience for fellow believers. Though the two positions—not speaking of evils and exposing them—might appear contradictory at first glance, the philosophical moralists indicate how the two can work together. Vices do not have to be named or spoken of in a community where they do not occur. Anyone who has mastered a subject no longer thinks of the lessons that were required in order to do so. For the ancient moralists the ethical life is best learned by imitation rather than verbal instruction. Nonetheless, verbal exhortation is needed. Such exhortation may take the mild form of reminder and encouragement as in Ephesians. Or it may take the harsh form of reprimand (as in 1 Cor

5:1-13, for example). The "wise" who serve as models for imitation do not need either type of parenesis. But they do have an obligation to instruct others. Ephesians has applied this model to the Christian life.

Wisdom as Thanksgiving (5:15-21)

This section opens as though it would conclude the parenesis. It combines a summons to conduct oneself wisely (vv. 15-18a) with a quasi-doxology (vv. 18b-20). An additional hortatory phrase (v. 21) permits the author to insert the Household Code (5:22–6:9) before the peroration (6:10-20). Ephesians 5:15-20 consists of a series of "not . . . but" clauses derived from material found in Colossians as the following table indicates:

Table 5: Eph 5:15-20 and Col 3:16-17; 4:5

Item	Ephesians	Colossians
not like the unwise	5:15 how you walk, not like the unwise but the wise	4:5 walk in wisdom toward those outside
the times are evil	5:16 employing the opportunity because the days are evil	4:5 employing the opportunity
forms of worship	5:19a speaking to one another in psalms and hymns and spiritual songs	3:16b instructing one another in all wisdom, singing psalms, hymns, spiritual songs
sing to God from the heart	5:19b singing and praising the Lord with your hearts	3:16c singing with thanks in your hearts to God
giving thanks to God	5:20 giving thanks always for all things in the name of our Lord	3:17 and everything whatever you do . . . all things in the name of

Jesus Christ to God	the Lord Jesus, giving
the Father	thanks to God the
	Father through him

Ephesians draws on other traditional material in verses 17*b*-18*a* (see Rom 12:2; Prov 23:31; *T. Jud.* 14.1). The two sections highlight the purposes for which the new community exists: praise of God's graciousness (1:6, 11) and walking in good works (2:10). "Filled with the Spirit" forms a transition between the sapiential "not . . . but" clauses and the worship section. On the one hand, "filled with the Spirit" serves as the antithesis to being drunken. On the other, the Spirit inspires worship and thanksgiving. Groups of three structure the material: (a) three "not . . . but" phrases (vv. 15*b*, 17-18); (b) three types of music (v. 19*a*); and (c) three participial phrases in the worship section: speaking to one another (v. 19*a*), singing and praising (v. 19*b*), and giving thanks (v. 20).

◊ ◊ ◊ ◊

The contrast between the wise and foolish (vv. 15-16) is common in wisdom material (see Prov 4:10-14). The Essenes internalized the feud between the Spirits of Light and Darkness as the contest between wisdom and folly, "Until now the spirits of truth and injustice feud in the heart of man and they walk in wisdom or in folly" (1QS 4:23-24). Though Ephesians does not speak of a contest between spiritual beings, it does reflect elements in the apocalyptic scheme. The warning "be careful how you live" highlights the constant danger that the righteous might be deceived in the present evil age. Essenes separate from "men of sin" by careful observance of the Law, "to convert from all evil and to keep themselves steadfast in all he prescribes in compliance with his will . . . those who persevere steadfastly in the covenant" (1QS 5:1, 4).

The Essene covenant community protects its members in an age ruled by Belial, "all those who enter in the Rule of the Community shall establish a covenant before God in order to carry out all that he commands and in order not to stray from following him for any fear, dread or grief that might occur during the dominion of Belial" (1QS 1:16-18). Ephesians makes a similar point in verse 16. The verb *exagorazein* (NRSV: "make the most of") means to purchase or to "buy back," that is, "redeem" something (as in Gal 3:13; 4:5). The meaning of the verb with the noun "time" is not clear. The Greek *kairos* ("time") can refer to a particular time, a favorable time, or even the time of crisis in an eschatological sense (as in Rom 13:11). Ephesians picks up the eschatological overtones of *kairos* by adding the clause "because the days are evil" (v. 16*b*). The expression suggests that the times themselves require one to be cautious (so Schnackenburg 1991).

The need for wisdom is intensified by the end-time perspective (vv. 17-18). While "drunkenness" and its resulting folly is a common item in vice lists (see Prov 23:29-35), the blindness or unconsciousness of a drunken humanity also appears as a metaphor in eschatological contexts (see 1 Thess 5:1-10; Rom 13:11-13). The antithesis "being drunk" or "being filled with the Spirit" has antecedents in the story of Hannah (1 Sam 1:12-18). Similarly, the crowd suspects the apostles of drunkenness on Pentecost (Acts 2:13; against this connection Lincoln 1990). There is no reason to assume that Ephesians speaks of abuses in the church (as was the case in 1 Cor 11:21-22; *pace* Schlier 1957; Gnilka 1980) or attraction to cultic orgies attached to a pagan god like Dionysus (*pace* Mussner 1982). The positive injunction "be filled with the Spirit" supports a chain of participles used as examples of Spirit-filled behavior.

Entry into the Essene covenant involved being cleansed of sin by the Spirit: "He will sprinkle over him the Spirit of Truth like lustral water (in order to cleanse him) from all the abhorrences of deceit and from the defilement of the unclean spirit" (1QS 4:21-22). Humans were divided according to which spirit ruled their hearts, "For God has sorted them into equal parts until the appointed end and the new creation . . . so they decide the lot of every living being in compliance with the spirit there is in him [at the time of] the visitation" (1QS 4:25-26). Likewise Christians received the Holy Spirit upon joining the church as the guarantee of their inheritance (Eph 1:12-14). The Spirit provides believers access to God (Eph 2:18) and dwells within them (Eph 3:16; 4:4).

Praise and thanksgiving (vv. 19-20) are the proper responses to what God has done in the believer (1:14; 3:20). Essene writers would agree that praising God is essential to the life of the righteous:

"He shall bless his Creator in all that transpires . . . [and with the offering] of his lips he shall bless him" (1QS 9:26). It is not possible to distinguish the various types of song referred to. Hymns and liturgical fragments are often cited in didactic contexts by New Testament authors (e.g., Phil 2:5-11; 1 Tim 3:16).

Since verse 21 introduces the Household Code material, some commentators treat it as the beginning of that section. However, the participle belongs in the chain begun earlier. The phrase "reverence for Christ" reflects the Old Testament "fear of God" (Ps 36:2 in Rom 3:18). Paul uses the verb *hupotassein* ("be subject") for obedience to rulers in Rom 13:5 (also 1 Pet 2:13; Titus 3:1). Some interpreters assume that Ephesians created verse 21 from the opening of the Household Code in Col 3:18. Others suggest that it represents a variant of New Testament exhortations to humility within the community (e.g., Rom 12:3, 10; Gal 6:2-3; Eph 4:2; Phil 2:3-4).

Essene writings provide another context in which the expression "submit" or "be subordinate" applies. Unity is a function of the ranks that members occupy: "No one shall move down . . . nor move up from the place of his lot. For all shall be in a single Community of truth, of proper meekness, of compassionate love and upright purpose, towards each other" (1QS 2:24-25). Order determined by the individual's insight and holiness governs relationships between members of the community, "each one obeys his fellow, junior under senior. And their spirit and their deeds must be tested year after year in order to upgrade one according to the extent of his insight and the perfection of his path. . . . Each should reproach his fellow in truth, in meekness and in compassionate love" (1QS 5:23-25). There is no such ranking in Ephesians. However, the Essene example also shows that "be subject to one another" is connected with virtues of humility and mutual correction as well as rank. Therefore the expression in Ephesians indicates how exhortation is to be conducted within the church.

◊ ◊ ◊ ◊

Both praise of God and conduct pleasing to the Lord require the assistance and participation of others. "Be subject to one another" as shorthand for the practice of mutual instruction and encouragement requires lives open to the observation and participation of others. Ephesians never forgets that believers are a single body in Christ. Its growth depends upon the well-being of all members. Mutual responsibility is particularly striking in churches like those addressed by Ephesians. The death of the apostles left others to carry on without the strong presence of an apostle-founder.

Believers must attend to their own conduct. Ephesians never suggests that such attention requires detailed moralism and legal observance. It does require consistent turning away from the old way of life. At the same time, this community exists as a worshiping community. Members must gather to offer praise and thanksgiving to God through Jesus Christ. Like their Jewish contemporaries, these Christians recognize that worshiping God and the blessing of God's presence in the Spirit are the keys to wisdom.

Household Code (5:22–6:9)

This section adopts a pattern of instruction on duties of household members from Col 3:18–4:1 (also see 1 Pet 2:18–3:7; Titus 2:1-10). The Stoic philosopher Hierocles detailed duties to gods, city, and household (see Malherbe 1986, 85-104). Other such descriptions occur in both Greco-Roman writers (e.g., Cicero *Off.* 1.17, 58; Dio Chrysostom *Orations* 4.91) and hellenistic Jewish ones (for example Pseudo-Phochylides 175-230; Philo *Post. Cain* 181). Seneca writes "how a husband should conduct himself towards his wife, or how a father should bring up his children, or how a master should rule his slaves, this department of philosophy is accepted by some as the only significant part" (Seneca *Epistles* 94.1; Malherbe 1986, 127). Comparative material extends back to Greek authors on household management (Aristotle *Politics* 1 1235^b 1-14; Xenophon *Oecon.*) and forward to neo-Pythagorean schools as well (see Dibelius and Greeven 1953, 48-50; Malherbe 1992, 304-13; Balch 1992).

Most scholars agree that the Household Code came to New Testament writers from hellenistic Jewish sources. Some exegetes detect an apologetic accommodation to larger social mores in the Household Codes. Conversion by inferior members of a household could be viewed as dangerous insubordination. The attention paid to women and slaves in 1 Peter suggests that such exemplary behavior is being recommended in order to ameliorate tensions that adherence to the new sect is causing (so Balch 1981).

A wisdom text from Qumran includes instruction for husbands and wives after comments on the appropriate honor due one's parents (4Q416 3:15-19, parents; 4:2, wife). The addressee is a poor person who might think that true piety is beyond his grasp. Unfortunately, the text is too fragmentary to determine what the sociological dynamics behind this reference to the addressee as poor might have been. The New Testament examples are atypical in addressing subordinate parties in the household first. In 1 Peter, a subsequent word to slave masters is lacking. That omission may reflect the socio-economic situation of its community.

Colossians 3:18–4:1 provides single sentence instructions for each group except slaves, where the advice is expanded to include obedience to the heavenly Lord. In taking over the material from Colossians, Ephesians reformulates it to indicate that all parties are Christian. The most striking interruption of the parallel clause form comes in the address to husbands (vv. 25-32). That digression concludes with a statement that addresses both husbands and wives (v. 33).

Since the other Christian Household Codes invoke Christ either as the Lord to whom obedience is paid (Col 3:23) or as model in suffering unjust treatment (1 Pet 2:18-25), the Christ and church application here probably originated as an example of subordination (Eph 5:23-24). Most conventional discourse on the topic of household management was addressed to males for whom harmonious governing of the household and ability to rule were closely related (see Balch 1981).

Table 6: Eph 5:22–6:9 as Household Code

Item	Ephesians	Colossians and other parallels
to wives	5:22 wives [be subject, from v. 21] to your own husbands as to the Lord	Col 3:18 wives, be subject to your husbands as is proper in the Lord

	5:33*b* let the wife respect her husband	1 Pet 3:1 likewise, wives be subject to your own husbands
		Titus 2:4-5 train young women to be loving of their husbands, loving of children . . . subject to their own husbands
reason for conduct	5:23-24 husband head of wife as Christ is head of church [his body, Christ its savior]; church subject to Christ, wife subject to husband in everything	[1 Cor 11:3 head of every man is Christ; head of a woman, her husband; head of Christ, God]
		Titus 2:5 that the word of God might not be slandered
		1 Pet 3:1*b*-2 unbelieving husbands may be won over without a word by reverent and chaste behavior
		[1 Pet 3:3-6 expansion: inner virtue to replace outward adornment; follow example of holy women such as Sarah; do right and have nothing to fear]
to husbands	5:25-27 husbands, love your wives, as Christ loved the church and gave himself up for her	Col 3:19 husbands, love your wives and do not be harsh with them
		1 Pet 3:7*a* likewise,

		husbands live considerately (with your wives) as the weaker vessel, bestowing honor on the woman
	[vv. 26-27 expansion: Christ cleanses church, presents her holy and unstained]	[Cf. 1 Pet 3:2-6, holiness of the virtuous wife]
	5:33a let each one love his wife as himself	
reason for conduct	5:28-32 therefore husbands ought to love their wives as their own bodies; the one who loves his wife loves himself, no one hates his own flesh, but nourishes and cherishes it as Christ does the church, because we are members of his body [cites Gen 2:24 exegical comment, vv. 31-32]	1 Pet 3:7b because you are fellow heirs of the grace of life, so that your prayers may not be hindered
to children	6:1 children, obey your parents in the Lord, for it is just	Col 3:20 children, obey your parents in everything for this is pleasing to the Lord
reason for conduct	6:2-3 cites Exod 20:12 + comment, "this is the irst commandment with a promise"	
to fathers	6:4 fathers, do not provoke your children to rage but nourish	Col 3:21 fathers, do not provoke your children

them with education
and knowledge of the
Lord

reason for conduct

lest they become
discouraged

to slaves

6:5-7 slaves obey your
lords according to the
flesh with fear and
trembling, in your
single heartedness, as to
Christ, not with eye-ser-
vice as pleasing people,
but as slaves of Christ,
Christ, doing the will
of God from the heart,
heart, serving with
zeal, as to the Lord
and not human beings

Col 3:22-23 slaves, obey
in all things your lords
according to the flesh,
not with eye-service as
pleasing people but in
single-heartedness,
fearing the Lord.
Whatever you do, work
from the heart as for the
Lord and not for human
beings

1 Pet 2:18 household
slaves, be subject in all
fear to your masters,
not only to the good
and gentle but also to
the harsh

Titus 2:9-10*a* slaves to be
subject *(hupotassesthai)*
to their own masters in
all things, to be pleasing,
not to be obstinate, not
thieving, but showing
complete, good
faithfulness

reason for conduct

6:8 knowing that each,
whatever good he does,
this he will get back
from the Lord, whether
slave or freeman

Col 3:24-25 knowing that
from the Lord, you will
receive back the reward
of the inheritance; you
serve the Lord Christ.

For the wicked will get back the wrong he has done, and there is no partiality

1 Pet 2:19 for this is as reason for gracious favor if in consciousness of God someone bears pains, suffering unjustly

[**2:20** explanation: no merit in enduring deserved punishment; God bestows favor on *(charis para theō)* those who do good and endure suffering]

[**2:21-25** example for imitation: Christ as suffering servant brought salvation from sin and healing]

Titus 2:10*b* so that in everything they may adorn the teaching of God our savior

to masters	**6:9***a* and lords, do the same things toward them, giving up the threat	**Col 4:1** lords, treat your slaves justly and equitably
reason for conduct	**6:9***b* knowing that their Lord and yours is in the heavens and there is no partiality with him	**Col 4:1***b* knowing that you also have a Lord in heaven [see **Col 3:25***b*]

Though attached to the exhortation of slaves, Col 3:25 constitutes an independent judgment saying, which may have been intended to refer to the unjust masters (so Barth and Blanke 1994). Ephesians 6:9 read Col 3:25 in that sense and relocated the warning about divine impartiality to the end of the saying addressed to the masters. Two levels of development are evident in the rest of the Household Code: first, Old Testament citations and comments to husbands (5:30-31) and children (6:2-3); second, the ecclesial imagery of Christ as head of the body (5:28-32; 1:22-23; 2:16; 3:6; 4:15-16, 25). The addition of Old Testament citations is independent of the "body of Christ" ecclesiology. First Peter uses Old Testament examples in its address to slaves and women. In the former case, Old Testament allusions are associated with Christ as suffering servant. In the latter, Sarah is the exemplary holy woman. Such developments suggest that the Household Code material was used in catechesis. The audience of Ephesians would recognize this section of parenesis as part of its own tradition.

◊ ◊ ◊ ◊

22-24: Verse 22 lacks a verb. The participle "being subject" can be supplied from verse 21. The same verb can be used for subjection to authorities and masters or for voluntary subordination on the part of those who might otherwise command respect (see *Arist.* 257; 1 Pet 5:5; Barth and Blanke 1994). The Household Codes presuppose that Christians will subordinate themselves to others as do the exhortations to obey civil authorities (Rom 13:1; Titus 3:1; 1 Pet 2:13). Of course, Christian women, slaves, or children cannot be subject to the religious opinions of husbands, masters, or parents if the latter oppose Christian faith.

Two parallel statements about the wife's subordination to her husband (vv. 23*a*, 24*b*) frame the two statements about the church (vv. 23*b*, 24*a*). The opening metaphor "husband is the head of the wife" echoes Paul's use of "head" for an order of hierarchical subordination in 1 Cor 11:3. Ephesians 5:23*b* refers Christ's position as "head" to his role as savior. The depiction of Christ's exaltation as head of the church in Eph 1:20-23 highlighted the cosmic dimensions of salvation. The question of how far to push the metaphor is raised by the juxtaposition of husband as head of his wife, with Christ as head of the church. Some interpreters point to 1:20-23 as evidence that the image should be referred to the power that Christ exercises on behalf of those who are members of his body. Others attempt to push the effect of the metaphor further. Insofar as the husband's authority is compared to that of Christ, the phrase "in everything" does not require wives to accept degrading or unworthy (i.e., unchristlike) forms of subjection.

Some commentators have seen this passage as evidence that Gnostic images of the spiritual marriage between the soul and the savior influenced Ephesians (Schlier 1957; Fischer 1973). Valentinian Gnostics enacted this mythological motif in a rite referred to as the "bridal chamber." That rite reversed the loss of humanity's original androgyny that occurred when Adam was divided from Eve. "His separation became the beginning of death. Because of this Christ came to repair the separation which was from the beginning and again unite the two, and to give life to those who died as a result. . . . But the woman is united to her husband in the bridal chamber" (*Gos. Phil.* 70,10-19).

Another Gnostic text refers to this section of Ephesians: "For they were originally joined to one another when they were with the father before the woman led astray the man, who is her brother. This marriage has brought them back together again and the soul has been joined to her true love, her real master, as it is written, 'For the master of the woman is her husband' " (*Exeg. Soul* 133,4-10). Other Gnostic texts speak of the church as a preexistent entity in the divine world *(pleroma)*. "Those which exist have come forth from the Son and the Father like kisses, . . . the kiss being a unity, although it involves many kisses. That is to say, it is the church consisting of many men that existed before the aeons, which is called in the proper sense "the aeon of aeons" (*Tri. Trac.* 58,22-33). The Savior's function is to restore the preexistent church to its original unity. Though it is easy to understand why these later Gnostic writers would read Ephesians as evidence for their views, the Epistle itself never suggests that the church as body of Christ preexists except in God's foreordained plan of salvation. Nor does Ephesians use the Gnostic imagery of the soul's reunion with her true spouse, returning instead to the traditional theology of the cross. Christ's death on the cross is the source of both the unity (2:14) and holiness (2:1-10; 5:2) of the church.

25-33: Ephesians begins the exhortation to husbands (vv. 25-33) with "love your wives" but omits the conventional "never treat them harshly" found in Col 3:19. Instead, Ephesians develops the body of Christ motif. Christ's self-sacrifice is a model to be imitated (Eph 5:2). Paul spoke of the local church as the pure bride of Christ (2 Cor 11:2). Ephesians assumes that Christ's death brought into being a church that is holy and unblemished. Some interpreters also find references to the bride of the Song of Songs (Cant 5:1; Bouttier 1991; Sampley 1971). "Washing of water by the word" refers to baptism (1 Cor 6:11; Titus 2:14; 3:5). The "word" was probably the name of Christ used during the ritual. Old Testament images might also be involved. Ezekiel 16:8-14 describes God bathing the battered nation, anointing and clothing her so that she can enter into a covenant with God whose glory she now shares. For Ephesians, the church now exists in holiness and glory. The church as "bride" does not depict the eschatological future as a wedding in the manner of Rev 19:5-10 (*pace* Barth 1974).

This extended description of the church as a bride prepared for the wedding highlights what has been accomplished by Christ's self-giving love. Husbands should love their wives with similar devotion. Ephesians does not imply that husbands are agents of holiness for their wives. Holiness comes to individual Christians through their incorporation into the body of Christ (*pace* Mussner 1982). However, the audience might assume that husbands are responsible for instructing their wives in holiness (cf. 1 Cor 14:34-35; 4Q416 Frag. 2 1:6-9).

Ephesians resumes with another development of the metaphor (vv. 28-30). The wife is like her husband's own body. A similar sentiment appears in Plutarch. He insists that the husband should not rule his wife in the way in which a master rules property but in the same way that the soul directs the body (Plutarch *Praec. Conj.* 142E). When Ephesians speaks of "nourishing" one's own flesh, the letter uses terms that would have been familiar to its audience. Ancient marriage contracts often included the husband's obligation to provide his wife with clothing and nourishment (Gnilka 1980). The conclusion returns to the activity of Christ. Conventional images continue to be transposed into the larger picture of the church's relationship to Christ. The author interrupts his presentation with another insertion of the "we" perspective (v. 30) so that the entire community is designated "Body of Christ."

Ephesians uses the term "mystery" here, as elsewhere, for the hidden purposes of God (v. 32; cf. 1:9; 3:3; 4:9; 6:19). The Essenes also speak of patient study of the Law as learning to perceive the mysteries (4Q416 Frag. 2 4:1). The quotation from Gen 2:24 appears in other contexts to bolster the prohibition of divorce (e.g., Mark 10:7-8). Essene legal codes use the related passage from Gen 1:27 in formulating their prohibition against divorce (CD 4:21). Ephesians may be familiar with the use of Gen 2:24 in such legal material. However, its exhortation to husbands gives no indication of addressing such issues.

Gnostic speculation regarded the division of Adam and Eve in Gen 2:23-24 as the source of death and human subjugation to the powers of the lower world. The savior comes to reveal that their true home lies above this world. The lost unity is restored when the soul is reunited with a heavenly counterpart. Consequently, Gnostic exegetes interpreted Gen 2:24 as Adam's recognition of the heavenly wisdom figure: "And Adam saw the woman beside him. In that moment the luminous Epinoia appeared, and she lifted the veil which lay over his mind. And he became sober from the drunkenness of darkness. And he recognized his counter-image, and he said, 'This is indeed bone of my bones and flesh of my flesh.' Therefore a man will leave his father and mother and cleave to his wife and they will both be one flesh. For they will send him his consort" (*Ap. John* II 23, 4-15). For the Gnostic interpreter the "mystery" involves liberation from the domination of the lower powers including the god of the Genesis story. For some, this freedom implied ascetic renunciation of all passions and desires, since passions were widely regarded as the means by which the demonic powers controlled human behavior. Other Gnostics of the Valentinian school assimilated human marriage to the "bridal chamber" reunification of the soul with its counterpart. This section of Ephesians appears in references to that ritual (see *Gos. Phil.* 64, 31-32). The term "mystery" refers to the Gnostic sacrament, "Indeed marriage in the world is a mystery for those who have taken a wife. If there is a hidden quality to the marriage of defilement, how much more is the undefiled marriage a true mystery!" (*Gos. Phil.* 82, 2-6).

These Gnostic texts exhibit a widespread concern over the passions that are involved in marriage. Paul's exchange with those in Corinth who viewed all sexuality as an obstacle to perfection provides an earlier example (1 Cor 7:1-31) of these passions. When faced with Christians who resorted to prostitutes, Paul used the dual images of belonging to the body of Christ and becoming "one flesh" with a sexual partner to argue the immorality of that behavior (1 Cor 6:12-20). He argued that marriage is an appropriate vehicle to "glorify God in your body" (6:20) against the radical ascetic view. Ephesians may have taken the "one flesh" language from earlier Pauline instruction, but it shows no concern with the practical issues that Paul was addressing in that earlier context. Nor does Ephesians move in the Valentinian direction of explaining Christian marriage as an image of the heavenly union that restores the soul to freedom from passions and death. Translation of the term "mystery" by the Latin *sacramentum* in some versions of the Old Latin and Vulgate traditions gave rise to use of this text in support of marriage as a Christian sacrament (Schnackenburg 1991).

Ephesians does not mythologize human marriage. Instead the text limits application of the "mystery" to the relationship between Christ and the church (v. 32). The earlier description of the growth of the body into its head through the activity of nerves, tendons, and joints (4:15-16) had established an organic relationship between Christ and the church. This "mystery" is another aspect of that saving reality.

The final verse brings the long digression back to the essential point of the exhortation, the relationship between husband and wife. It reaffirms the hierarchical view of marriage and the household in ancient times. Modern translations prefer the more neutral term "respect" for the "fear" or "reverence" (*phobētai*) required of the wife. The ancient author and his readers would presume that she, like all other members of the household, is subject to the authority of its male head. The term "fear" can be used of all social relationships in which subordination is involved. On the other hand, the relationship between husband and wife is different from that between the husband/master and his slaves. The relationship between husband and wife modeled upon Christ's self-sacrificing love indicates a constant concern on the husband's part for her well-being that is not part of other hierarchical relationships in the household.

6:1-4: Ephesians returns in 6:1-4 to the traditional shorter exhortation. The Essene example indicates that "children" refers to adults obliged to care for and respect aging parents, "Honour your father in your poverty and your mother in your steps, for like grass for a man, so is his father, and like a pedestal for a man, so is his mother. For they are the oven of your origin, and just as they have dominion over you and form the spirit, so you must serve them" (4Q416 Frag. 2 col. 3:16-17). Paul used the obligations of adult children toward their parents to describe relationships between himself and his converts. Paul refuses material support despite his needs. Rather, he insists that the Corinthians show him the love due a father (2 Cor 11:9; Yarbrough 1995). As a solicitous father, Paul seeks to present the community to Christ as a pure bride (2 Cor 11:2).

The Old Testament citation (vv. 2*a*, 3) is closer to LXX Exod 20:12 than to Deut 5:16. The conviction that the Law teaches its followers "what is right" appears in Jewish apologetic. Attacks on paganism described the evil of disobedient children as the result of idolatry (Rom 1:29-31). This section affirms a conventional understanding of the appropriate relationship between children and parents. Some philosophers admit that children should disobey a father who tried to prohibit the study of philosophy (Barth and Blanke 1994).

Ephesians focuses on the requirement that parents educate their children (v. 4). The Essene example used the education received from parents as the basis for the obligation of adult children toward their parents. A treatise attributed to Plutarch argues that training one's children in philosophy will guarantee the social conformity that is the object of the Household Code parenesis. The author writes, "Through philosophy . . . it is possible to attain knowledge of what is just and unjust . . . that one ought to reverence the gods, to honor one's parents, . . . to be obedient to the laws, to yield to those in authority, to love one's friends, to be chaste with women, to be affectionate with children, and not to be overbearing with slaves" (Pseudo-Plutarch *Education of Children* 7DE; Malherbe 1986, 30-31). Parental affection toward, and education of, children appear in Paul's use of parent-child imagery to describe his relationship to the churches he founded (1 Thess 2:7-12; 1 Cor 4:14-21; Yarbrough 1995).

Sirach 30:1-13 recommends strict discipline, constant correction, and beating so that the son will become like his father. However, warnings against excessive harshness can also be found. The Pseudo-Plutarch treatise, for example, contrasts the education of freeborn children to that of slaves. Beating is for slaves. Exhortation, reasoning, and encouragement should be used for children (Pseudo-Plutarch *Education of Children* 8F; also Pseudo-Phocylides 207).

Ephesians is less interested in the negative aspects of discipline than the positive responsibility for instruction. The term "discipline" (Gk. *paideia*) spans the range between appropriate discipline for young children to the philosophical instruction of the older adolescent (Sir 1:27 connects "fear of the Lord, *paideia*, and wisdom"). The second term "instruction" refers to verbal correction or education. Thus Ephesians indicates that Christian fathers will be devoted to training their children in virtuous behavior.

5-9: The instruction to slaves (vv. 5-8) is more lengthy than that given the other subordinate groups. As Table 6 indicated, this material is an adaptation of Col 3:22-25. The conventional Christian modification (slaves serve the Lord, not just human masters) remains. Discussion of how slaves are to be treated appears in all ancient codes (Balch 1992, 405-6). The New Testament codes are distinctive in addressing slaves directly rather than merely providing rules to the master. Slaves were members of early Christian communities (Gal 3:28; Philemon; 1 Cor 7:20-24). Ancient authors often depicted slaves as unreliable, groveling and fawning on masters whom they secretly despise. If the master relaxes his stern discipline or turns his back, slaves become disobedient, steal from the household, and deserve punishment (cf. Luke 12:41-48). The virtuous slave depicted in the Christian Household Code is not to be lumped with such cultural stereotypes. His or her dignity lies in service to the Lord (Barth and Blanke 1994). An owner might free, in his will, those slaves whom he considered zealous and affectionate (*POxy* 494.6; Lincoln 1990). Ephesians shifts that possibility of human reward for devoted service to the Lord who governs the behavior of all Christians regardless of their status (v. 8).

Judgment brings the slave and master under the same Lord. The warning that Col 3:25 addressed to wicked slaves has been reformulated in Eph 6:8, which speaks of the Lord rewarding each person, slave or free, for any good they do. The reminder that God is an impartial judge appears at the end reinforcing this admonition to masters. The partiality that power and position gave individuals in human courts does not apply in front of the heavenly judge (cf. Rom 2:10-11; 2 Cor 5:10). Though the warning addressed to masters appears stronger than that in Col 4:1, the imperatives are weaker. Instead of the positive characteristics—just and equitable treatment—required of masters in Colossians, Eph 6:9*a* has an unclear admonition to "do the same" and avoid threatening behavior. The latter reflects a common theme in master/slave relationships: the injuries that result from a master's rage. Consequently, philosophers exhort masters to avoid anger in dealing with slaves (Seneca *Ira* 3.24.2; 32.1). A female Pythagorean philosopher, Theano, directs similar advice on treatment of household slaves to young wives. They must avoid mistreating slaves through excessive toil and must restrain the cruel temper that some people exhibit in punishing slaves (Balch 1992, 405). Thus the behavior required of Christian slave-owners does not differ appreciably from that enjoined by hellenistic moralists. The difference appears in the motive clauses. The eschatological understanding that the Lord in the heavens treats all alike undermines a fundamental assumption in the hierarchy of power, that those in power enjoy their position through divine favor (Bouttier 1991).

◊ ◊ ◊ ◊

COMMENTARY

Christians today often find the Household Code ethic an awkward accommodation to cultural patterns that would be considered unjust or, in the case of slavery, immoral. First-century readers of Ephesians would find its concern for proper roles and subordination quite natural. Women were expected to defer to their husbands. Adult children continued to be subject to the authority of their parents. In that context, Ephesians directs those in authority to moderate common forms of abusive power. The father's authority over wife and children requires self-sacrifice for their welfare. It does not permit subjecting them to dehumanizing labor or harsh punishments. Ephesians 5:22-33 contains a unique development of the traditional ethic in the extended description of the husband's love and concern for his wife.

Ephesians presumes households in which both dominant and subordinant parties share a common faith unlike the situation in 1 Peter where wives and slaves are subject to non-Christians. Since the household was considered the fundamental unit of the larger society, the relationship of Christians to the larger social structures is also at stake. Both Rom 13:1-7 and 1 Pet 2:13-17 incorporate the piece on civic hierarchy and concord that pertains to Greco-Roman treatments of household management.

Most exegetical attempts to detect some radical modification of the ethical injunctions based on special Christian insight or compassion fail to prove their case. Guiding images and motivational statements have been shaped by Christian language and views of the world. But the content and social implications of this parenesis are not peculiar to the Christian variants. What is the significance of the early Christian appropriation of such ethical commonplaces? Does it lend the authority of Scripture to a particular sociocultural understanding of order or of family? Does the fact that the initial impetus for use of such material may have been apologetic or used to lessen the tensions between converts and those on whom they depended make the material irrelevant in another setting? Ephesians, which gives no evidence of the problems addressed in 1 Peter, would seem to counter that view. For Ephesians this ethic describes a well-ordered Christian household independent of the views or actions of outsiders.

Peroration: Be Armed with the Power of God (6:10-20)

The final section of the letter returns to the theme of divine power introduced in its opening section (1:19-21). Christ has triumphed over powers at work in the present age (1:21; 2:2; 3:10). His exaltation provides the energy at work in believers and in the ministry of the imprisoned apostle (3:7). Ephesians 6:10-20 is the peroration that brings the letter to a rhetorical conclusion (so Lincoln 1995).

The unit falls into three sections. Verses 10-13 contain an opening statement and the command to take up God's weaponry against the hostile spiritual powers (see 2:2; 4:27). Verses 14-17 link items of divine armor with virtues or gifts of salvation. Finally, verses 18-20 return to the theme of prayer. This prayer asks that the imprisoned apostle continue his bold witness to the mystery of salvation (vv. 19-20; cf. 3:1-13). Readers know the content of the "mystery of the gospel" (v. 19; from 1:9; 3:3, 4, 9; 5:32). By enlisting their prayers on behalf of the apostle, Eph 6:18-20 indicates that the discourse has brought its audience to maturity as members of the body of Christ.

The call to battle marks a striking departure from the realized eschatology of exaltation above the heavenly powers, which suggested that the victory was already won. Andrew T. Lincoln detects an emotional appeal similar to those calls to battle that were composed for famous generals in the histories of the time (e.g., Cyrus in Xenophon *Cyrop.* 1.4; Hannibal and Scipio in Polybius 3.63; Anthony and Augustus in Dio Cassius *History* 1.16-30; Lincoln 1995). If verses 10-17 are the general's call to battle, what is the rhetorical impact of the shift in verses 18-20? The general-orator is already in chains (v. 20)! Suddenly the image has shifted from armed soldier to the bold martyr able to disregard the threats of soldiers arrayed against him (cf. 2 Macc 7).

Both the image of the conquering general and that of the bold prisoner have antecedents in the Pauline letters. As prisoner, Paul testifies to imperial guards (Phil 1:12-14) and even fights with the beasts (1 Cor 15:32; a metaphorical expression for the hardships endured while preaching in Ephesus). As general, the apostle lays siege to those who resist knowledge of Christ with powers provided by God (2 Cor 10:3-6; Malherbe 1983). One may compare how first-century Cynic and Stoic philosophers spoke of the invulnerability of a wise man's soul when fortified by reason and secure virtue, "full of virtues human and divine, [the wise man] can lose nothing. . . . The walls which guard the wise man are safe from both flame and assault, they provide no means of entrance, are lofty, impregnable, godlike" (Seneca *Const. Sap.* 6.8; Malherbe 1986, 160). Cynics referred to their rough garb as armor in the war against the temptations of a soft life, lovers, false opinions, or other forms of cultural imprisonment (Pseudo-Diogenes *Epistles* 34). Dio argued that the philosopher's true weapons are words, not beggarly forms of dress (Dio Chrysostom *Orations* 19.10-12). Paul, however, does not give any description of the weapons that he uses, saying only that his weapons "have divine power to destroy" (2 Cor 10:4). The weapons appear to be the lowly form of life that his opponents have used as evidence against him (2 Cor 10:7-10; Malherbe 1983).

Second Corinthians 10:1-10 provides an indication that the general's call to arms and the bold prisoner image could be combined in describing the apostle. The apparent humiliation of imprisonment may even form part of the attack. The combination speaks eloquently to the rhetorical situation of the audience. Ephesians hints that imprisonment (and perhaps already death) has removed the apostle from the field. However, its readers are ready to take up the arms provided by God.

Details of divine armor do not occur in the earlier letters. First Thessalonians 5:8 picks two pieces of armor as metaphors: for the virtues of faith and love, the breastplate; and for hope of salvation, the helmet. Ephesians 6:14-17 must have created its picture of the armor from other sources. The closest parallels appear in descriptions from Isaiah as the following table indicates.

Table 7: Eph 6:14-17 and the Armor of the Lord

Item	Ephesians	Isaiah and other parallels
belt ("having girded your loins")	**6:14** truth	**Isa 11:5** (LXX) righteousness

breastplate	6:14 righteousness	Isa 59:17 (LXX) righteousness (also **Wis 5:18**)
military sandals ("having shod your feet")	6:15 equipment of the gospel of peace	[Isa 52:7 (LXX) "the feet of those who preach the tidings of peace"]
shield	**6:16** faith	**Wis 5:19** holiness
helmet	**6:17** salvation	Isa 59:17 (LXX) salvation
		Wis 5:18 impartial judgment
sword	**6:17** the Spirit, which is the word of God	[**Isa 49:2** (LXX) placed in the mouth of the servant "a sharp sword"]
		Wis 5:20 "wrath as a large sword"

A blessing of the "prince of the congregation" at Qumran also uses battle imagery to establish the new covenant: "He will renew the covenant . . . to establish the kingdom of his people forever [to judge the poor with justice]. . . ." This individual will be a fortress: "May the Lord raise you to an everlasting height, like a fortified tower upon the raised rampart." The word of his mouth is a sharp weapon: "May [you strike the peoples] with the power of your mouth. . . . With the breath of your lips may you kill the wicked." And he will be clad in armor: "May your justice be the belt [of your loins, and loyalty] the belt of your hips. May he place upon you horns of iron and horseshoes of bronze" (1Q28b 5:21-26).

Use of the Isaiah material in Wisdom and 1Q28b shows that the metaphor did not include a fixed set of correlations between armor and virtues. The blessing of the Prince of the Congregation from Qumran also indicates that the armor of the Lord can be transferred from God to human agents. Both Qumran and Ephesians refer to this armor without any citation formulae. Both assume that the audience will recognize the biblical cast of the imagery. Such recognition plays an important part in the linguistic code of each document. In the Essene text, God's blessing on the leader of the renewed covenant people equips him to be the agent of divine justice and judgment among the peoples. In Ephesians the enemies to be resisted are no longer human but spiritual, quasi-demonic powers that govern the lower world. God's armor expresses the superior power of the creator already evident in the exaltation of Christ into the heavens. The philosophical tradition of the sage armed against the passions and false reasonings of humankind would not be sufficient in either context.

◊ ◊ ◊ ◊

10-13: The introduction in verse 10 echoes Col 1:11. A call to be vigilant frequently appears in apocalyptic conclusions. Readers know God's power in the salvation that they have already experienced (1:19; 3:16, 30). Wearing the soldier's armor (v. 11; from Wis 5:17) presents a more striking metaphor for divine protection than the earlier references to divine power. Though the concrete details of the armor are biblical, not Roman, the audience probably envisaged the fully armed Roman soldier when they heard these words (Polybius 6.23; Jdt 14:3; 2 Macc 3:25; Lincoln 1990).

The idea that Satan has designs on the righteous is familiar (2:2). The parenesis warned against permitting anger to provide opportunities for the devil (4:27), but the catalogue of powers in verse 12 has been a source of controversy since antiquity. Gnostic authors used Eph 6:12 as evidence that the soul is trapped in a world created by the evil creator and his subordinate powers. One account of this mythology is introduced as the revelation of the meaning of the apostle's words: "On account of the reality of the authorities inspired by the spirit of the father of truth, the great apostle referring to the 'authorities of darkness' [Col 1:13] told us that 'our contest is not against flesh and [blood]; rather, the authorities of the universe and the spirits of wickedness [Eph 6:12]" (*Hyp. Arch.* 86,20-25). Gnostic mythology gave more explicit expression to the hints in Ephesians that God has already given victory to the elect (Lindemann 1975, 655).

Other exegetes have taken the peculiar term "cosmic powers" as evidence that Ephesians refers to the powers behind astrology and magic (Arnold 1987). In inscriptions "cosmic power" implies that the deity invoked is omnipotent and universal. Use of the term in the plural is unusual, and Clinton Arnold contends that Ephesians wishes to demote Artemis and other deities in so doing. They are not universal rulers but members of the lower class of powers referred to as demons. Paul agrees that the pagan gods can be described as demons (1 Cor 10:20).

While the terms "ruler" and "authority" are frequently found in the New Testament (Eph 1:21; 3:10), the expressions "cosmic powers" and "spiritual forces of evil in the heavenly places" seem to have been coined by the author of Ephesians. They are equivalent to other descriptions of evil powers in Jewish apocalyptic (*Jub.* 10:3-13; *1 Enoch* 15:8-12; *T. Sim.* 4:9). By expanding the double expression "rulers and authorities" with these new terms, Ephesians has conveyed a sense that powers of evil pervade the cosmos. However, God's power is superior to any such forces. The expression found in verse 10 ("in the strength of his power") could be an allusion to Isa 40:26 (LXX) "in the strength of might." Isaiah refers to the creative power of God in bringing forth the universe and its heavenly bodies (Wild 1984).

Verse 13 picks up the exhortation of verse 11. Given the strength of the forces arrayed against them, Christians must be well armed to withstand the day of battle. What does Ephesians mean by the expression "that evil day"? Possibilities range from the evils of the time just before the end, particular instances of temptation, or simply everyday life in the present age. The apocalyptic background of much of the imagery makes a reference to end-time evil seem the most natural (cf. 1 Cor 7:26; 1 Thess 5:2-4). Elsewhere in Ephesians, however, apocalyptic expressions are usually converted to descriptions of present reality (so Schnackenburg 1991; see 1:21; 2:3, 7; 1:14, 18; 4:30; 5:5). The vagueness of the concluding clause, "having done everything, to stand firm," suggests that the author has an indefinite future in mind. The structures of the present age will continue for an unknown period. The phrase does not specify what is meant by "having done everything." It could refer to having put on the armor or to having resisted the enemy when under attack.

14-17: Verse 14 picks up the verb "stand" from the end of the previous sentence. A series of participles describe those standing as properly equipped with each piece of armor (vv. 14-17). As Table 7 indicates, the equipment and characteristics associated with the various items of armor have been taken from traditions concerning the armor of the Lord. Although the previous verses suggested that the combat was primarily defensive, most of the virtues in this section speak of positive actions. Such offensive acts bring the image closer to that of the Lord arming himself to come in judgment or to the Essene Prince of the Congregation ready to establish the new people of God. When Eph 4:24 uses the verb "clothe" for the new human being created in God's image, that new being is created in righteousness and holiness of truth. Righteousness, goodness, and truth are fruits of light (5:9). Thus, virtues that Christians have "put on" when they were converted provide the desired armor. Military-style hobnailed sandals or short boots used as equipment for the gospel of peace suggest readiness for a long march if readers associate the image with Isa 52:7. Romans 10:15 uses the same passage as Isaiah for messengers of the gospel. For Ephesians, the peace that comes through preaching the gospel is constituted by the unity of Jew and Gentile in the body of Christ (2:14, 17).

Since verse 16 refers to withstanding an attack, some commentators reject the possibility that preaching the gospel is being referred to in verse 15 (so Lincoln 1990). Others suggest that the expression ("whatever will make you ready to proclaim the gospel of peace") refers to the soldier as armed to do battle in order to preserve a peace that has already been established, not to create that peace (Schnackenburg 1991). Ephesians speaks of peace as given by God's plan of salvation, harmoniously uniting all things in heaven and on earth in Christ (1:10). This plan has already been made known to the "rulers and authorities" in the heavens (3:10).

Unlike the small round shield (Gk. *aspis*), the *thureos* was a full-length shield of leather-covered wood that protected the whole body (Polybius 6.23; Lincoln 1990). Burning arrows have been used in attacks on besieged cities since Assyrian times. A soldier who became terrified by flaming arrows caught in his shield might throw it down and become vulnerable to enemy spears (Thucydides *The Peloponnesian War* 2.75,5). For the audience these familiar images must also be linked to the use of "shield" for God (Gen 15:1; Pss 5:12; 18:30; 28:7) and to the arrows and sword God has readied for the wicked (Ps 7:12-13; Isa 50:11).

Arrows appear as metaphors for sins of speech (Prov 26:18). The blasphemous words that the wicked speak against God are fiery arrows that eventually ignite divine wrath (CD 5:12-16; 1QH 11[= 3]:16, 27). The closest parallel to the image in Ephesians can be found in one of the Essene hymns. The righteous person, the speaker in this hymn, trusts in the Lord despite the attacks being mounted against him: "They—they attack my life on your account, so that you will be honored by the judgment of the wicked . . . heroes have set up camp against me surrounded by all their weapons of war; they loose off arrows without any cure; the tip of the spear, like fire which consumes trees" (1QH 10:23-26). It is the speaker's testimony to the truth about God that excites the attack of the wicked: "You have set me as a reproach and a mockery of traitors, foundation of truth and of knowledge for those on the straight path" (1QH 10[= 2]:10). Ephesians has already indicated that "the ruler of the power of the air" is the spirit working in the "those who are disobedient" (2:2). Therefore the fiery arrows of the evil one might represent the speech of the wicked. If Ephesians makes the same associations with fiery darts that the Essene hymnist does, then the earlier reference to the "gospel of peace" should be taken in an active sense. The message conveyed by the faithful about God's salvation provokes the assaults that they suffer.

The active imagery returns in verse 17, which highlights offensive weapons. Along with the helmet, the faithful are encouraged to take up the sword that is the word of God. "Sword" refers to the short sword used in close combat. Ordinarily, the metaphor refers to the sword that comes from God's mouth to strike down his enemies (also Rev 1:16; 2:12, 16; 19:13, 15). In this context, "word" must refer to the Christian message, the gospel (as in Rom 10:8; 1 Pet 1:25).

18-20: Ephesians concludes the peroration by returning to the theme of prayer that opened the letter (vv. 18-20). The formula has been appropriated from Col 4:2-4. By turning the reader's attention back to the imprisoned apostle, the dramatic emotional impact of the call to arms is softened. The author now appeals to the audience's emotions. They should be eager to follow the example of the heroic apostle that has been set before them. Ephesians has already indicated that prayer is necessary for those who would receive divine power (1:15-23; 3:14-21). Exhortations and references to continual prayer are a regular feature of Pauline letters (Phil 1:4; 4:6; 1 Thess 5:17; Rom 1:9-10; Col 1:3; 4:12). The phrase "for all the saints" reminds the audience of its ties to all believers (1:15; 3:18). Prayer is regularly described as the activity of the Spirit in the believer (Gal 4:6; Rom 8:15-16, 26-27).

Philippians speaks of the effects of Paul's imprisonment. It has made others confident in preaching the gospel (Phil 1:14-16). The prayers offered on his behalf by the Philippians can be credited with delivering the apostle from prison—along with the agency of the Spirit (Phil 1:19-20). The prayer formula at the conclusion to Ephesians has generalized this pattern. One can no longer anticipate that the apostle will be freed from prison. Ephesians even omits the reference to an "open door" for proclaiming the gospel from Col 4:3. However, the addressees can share Paul's courageous testimony to the gospel through praying for him.

The self-description of the apostle as "ambassador in chains" (v. 20) has taken the term "serve as ambassador" from 2 Cor 5:20. Philemon 9 combines the terms "ambassador" and "prisoner." The reference to chains appears elsewhere in Acts 28:20 and 2 Tim 1:16. Both the weight and manner of chaining prisoners made chains extremely painful. Coupled with lack of nourishment, such imprisonment could result in permanent damage to the prisoner's limbs. Because of the physical torture involved in being chained, later legislation referred to slavery and low social rank as "the punishment of bonds" (Rapske 1994, 206-9). When the realities of prison are grasped clearly, the suggestion that the apostle would continue to boldly proclaim the gospel is more evidently heroic than is the case for readers who think only of modern prisons. The prison context also indicates that to speak of an ambassador in chains would be considered an oxymoron (Lincoln 1990). A wretched, dirty creature in chains could hardly make the rhetorical show necessary to accomplish the task of ambassador. Nevertheless both Philippians and Philemon indicate that Paul did manage to use imprisonment as an opportunity to spread the gospel. This section indicates that he will continue to do so.

◊ ◊ ◊ ◊

Much of the drama of this peroration depends upon the range of emotional associations that an audience attaches to the rich imagery that makes up the passage. Life as a combat with astral powers located in the lower regions of the air has been coupled with believers putting on the armor of the divine warrior himself. Swords and arrows will not be effective against such weapons. But the tone of victory may be swept away when Ephesians shifts to the imprisoned apostle. Though the harsh conditions of imprisonment would seem to make witness to the gospel impossible, Philemon demonstrates that Paul might even convert fellow prisoners.

Ephesians does not suggest that its readers are about to be imprisoned as Paul is. But the world in which they live is not going to be transformed. Hostile powers still govern the present age. They may attack the saints through the fiery arrows of verbal polemic. At one level, the armor appears to be equivalent to the new clothing that Christians put on when they are converted. At another, as the parenetic section of the letter indicates, preparation to withstand attack must be continuous. Believers must hear sermons, read scripture, talk with other Christians, engage in regular prayer, sing the praises of God, and so on.

Ancient philosophers highlight the connection between open or bold speech and freedom. Someone who has a secure grasp on his or her identity as a believer cannot be forced to surrender that truth. The armed soldier of this section provides an image of the secure believer. Such persons cannot be found shifting from one opinion to another, "tossed to and fro and blown about by every wind . . . by their craftiness in deceitful scheming" (4:14); their position should instead be "speaking the truth in love" (4:15).

FINAL GREETING (6:21-24)

Ancient letters ended with information about the sender's immediate plans, additional instructions, or words to particular individuals. Since Ephesians is not addressed to an audience that knew Paul personally, such concrete details are lacking. By contrast, Colossians ends with an extended list of greetings and instructions to named individuals (Col 4:10-17). Ephesians has taken wording for the final greeting from Colossians, as the following table indicates.

Table 8: Eph 6:21-24 and Col 4:7-9, 18

Item	Ephesians	Colossians
information about the sender	**6:21** and that you may know how I am and what I am doing,	**4:7** how I am doing,
person who brings the letter	**6:21b** Tychicus, the beloved brother, faithful minister in the Lord will make everything known to you	**4:7b** Tychicus, the beloved brother, faithful minister, and fellow servant in the Lord will make everything known to you
recommendation for the bearer	**6:22** whom I have sent to you for this purpose, that you may know how we are doing, and to be encouraged in your hearts	**4:8** whom I have sent to you for this purpose, that you may know how we are doing and be encouraged in your hearts
final blessing	**6:23-24** Peace to the brothers, and love with	**4:18** I, Paul, write the greeting with my own

faith, from God the
Father and the Lord
Jesus Christ. Grace
with all who love our
Lord Jesus Christ
in incorruptibility.

hand. Remember my
bonds. Grace be with
you.

The final words diverge from Colossians. Ephesians does not conclude in the apostle's own hand (as do Gal 6:11; Phlm 19) and the reference to Paul's imprisonment has been relocated to the peroration (v. 20).

◊ ◊ ◊ ◊

In Colossians the double reference to how Paul is doing (4:7) and how "we are" doing (4:8) makes sense because Col 1:1 identified Timothy as co-sender of the letter. There is no co-sender in Eph 1:1, but its author has retained the second plural reference anyway. Tychicus appears in Acts 20:4 as one of Paul's companions from Asia Minor. His name reappears in the pastorals as emissary to Ephesus and Crete (2 Tim 4:12; Titus 3:12). The notice that connected Tychicus and Ephesus provides a basis for the speculation—appearing in those manuscripts that add the phrase "in Ephesus" to the opening (1:1)—that this general letter was addressed to Christians in Ephesus.

The final greeting (vv. 23-24) expands the short form found in Colossians somewhat awkwardly. Its structure reflects the "grace to you and peace from God our Father and the Lord Jesus Christ" of the opening greeting (1:2). The expression "love with faith" is unusual as is the lack of a vocative or a second person plural for those who are the object of the concluding blessing. Instead of personal greetings, Ephesians employs generalized expressions: "peace to the brothers" (NRSV: "the whole community") and "grace be with all who have an undying love for our Lord Jesus Christ." Consequently, any Christians who happen upon the letter may feel themselves included as its addressees. This form of address may indicate that Ephesians was composed as a circular letter.

The letter's final prepositional phrase "in incorruptibility" (translated as the adjectival "undying" in the NRSV) is awkward.

One might expect the term "incorruptibility" to describe a divine attribute (Rom 1:23; 1 Tim 1:17). If so, the phrase refers to the Lord exalted in incorruptibility. But one would expect a verbal form to connect "the Lord" with the prepositional phrase or the adjective modifying that word. Therefore the phrase probably modifies the verb "love" as in the NRSV. It asserts that love of Christ is not subject to decay. This reading is grammatically clearer, though it still yields an awkward expression. First Corinthians 15:42 uses the prepositional phrase to describe the risen body. A formulaic passage in 2 Tim 1:10 speaks of Christ abolishing death and bringing to light life and incorruptibility through the gospel. These examples show that if "in incorruptibility" refers to believers, "incorruptibility" should refer to their eschatological situation, not the quality of their love of the Lord. Perhaps Ephesians is referring to those who love the Lord as the church that exists with him "in the heavenly places" (2:6-7). Its existence is the result and evidence of the richness of God's grace toward those who believe. Thus the author indirectly returns to one of the great themes of the letter. The existence of the church, united in love with its head, is the sign of God's loving providence. God wills to unite all people in the new creation. Like all divine attributes, the response to God's grace— love for the Lord Jesus—is also incorruptible.

SELECT BIBLIOGRAPHY

WORKS CITED IN THE TEXT
(EXCLUDING COMMENTARIES)

Abrahamsen, Valerie A. 1995. *Women and Worship at Philippi: Diana/ Artemis and Other Cults in the Early Christian Era*. Portland, ME: Astarte Shell.

Arnold, Clinton E. 1987. "The 'Exorcism' of Ephesians 6.12 in Recent Research: A Critique of Wesley Carr's View of the Rule of Evil Powers in First-Century AD Belief." *JSNT* 30:71-87.

———. 1989. *Ephesians: Power and Magic: The Concept of Power in Ephesians in the Light of its Historical Setting*. SNTSMS 63. Cambridge: Cambridge University Press.

Augustine. 1992. *Confessions*. Translated by Henry Chadwick. Oxford: Oxford University Press.

Balch, David L. 1981. *Let Wives Be Submissive: The Domestic Code in 1 Peter*. SBLMS 26. Atlanta: Scholars Press.

———. 1992. "Neopythagorean Moralists and the New Testament Household Codes." In *Aufstieg und Niedergang der römischen Welt* II 26/1, edited by Wolfgang Haase, 380-411. Berlin: DeGruyter.

Barth, Markus, and Helmut Blanke. 1994. *Colossians*. AB 34B. New York: Doubleday.

Barton, Tamsyn. 1994. *Ancient Astrology*. London/New York: Routledge.

Belleville, Linda L. 1991. *Reflections of Glory: Paul's Polemical Use of the Moses-Doxa Tradition in 2 Corinthians 3.1-18*. JSNTSup 52. Sheffield: JSOT.

Best, Ernest. 1987. "Recipients and Title of the Letter to the Ephesians: Why and When the Designation 'Ephesians'?" In *Aufstieg und Niedergang der römischen Welt* II 25/4, edited by Wolfgang Haase, 3247-79. Berlin: DeGruyter.

Betz, Hans Dieter. 1979. *Galatians*. Philadelphia: Fortress.

———. 1995. *The Sermon on the Mount*. Minneapolis: Fortress.

———, ed. 1986. *The Greek Magical Papyri in Translation*. Vol. 1, *Texts*. Chicago: University of Chicago Press.

Cargal, Timothy B. 1994. " 'Seated in the Heavenlies': Cosmic Mediators in the Mysteries of Mithras and the Letter to the Ephesians." In SBLSP, edited by Eugene H. Lovering, 804-21. Atlanta: Scholars Press.

Charlesworth, James H., ed. 1983–85. *OTP*. Vol. 1, *Apocalyptic Literature and Testaments*. Vol. 2, *Expansions of the "Old Testament" and Legends, Wisdom and Philosophical Literature, Prayers, Psalms, and Odes, Fragments of Lost Judeo-Hellenistic Works*. Garden City, NY: Doubleday.

Collins, John. 1993. *Daniel*. Minneapolis: Fortress.

Dillon, John. 1977. *The Middle Platonists*. London: Duckworth.

Dimant, Devorah. 1992. "Pesharim, Qumran." In *ABD Volume 5O—Sh*, edited by David Noel Freedman, 244-51. New York: Doubleday, 1992.

Dunn, James D. G. 1980. *Christology in the Making: A New Testament Inquiry into the Origins of the Doctrine of the Incarnation*. Philadelphia: Westminster.

———. 1995. "The Colossian Philosophy: A Confident Jewish Apologetic." *Bib* 76:153-81.

Evans, Craig A. 1984. "The Meaning of *plērōma* in Nag Hammadi." *Bib* 65:259-65.

Faust, Eberhard. 1993. *Pax Christi et Pax Caesaris. Religionsgeschichtliche, traditionsgeschichtliche und sozial geschichtliche Studien zum Epheserbrief*. NTOA, 24. Freiburg: Universitätsverlag; Göttingen: Vandenhoeck & Ruprecht.

Fee, Gordon D. 1994. *God's Empowering Presence: The Holy Spirit in the Letters of Paul*. Peabody, MA: Hendrickson.

Feldman, Louis H. 1993. *Jew and Gentile in the Ancient World*. Princeton, NJ: Princeton University Press.

Fischer, Karl Martin. 1973. *Tendenz und Absicht des Epheserbriefes*. FRLANT 111. Göttingen: Vandenhoeck & Ruprecht.

Fitzmyer, Joseph A. 1993. *Romans*. AB 33. New York: Doubleday.

García Martínez, Florentino. 1994. *The Dead Sea Scrolls Translated: The Qumran Texts in English*. Leiden: E. J. Brill.

Georgi, Dieter. 1995. "The Early Church: Internal Jewish Migration or New Religion?" *HTR* 88:35-68.

Goldingay, John E. 1989. *Daniel*. WBC 30. Dallas: Word.

Goodman, Martin. 1994. *Mission and Conversion: Proselytizing in the Religious History of the Roman Empire*. Oxford: Clarendon.

Gouldner, Michael. 1994. "Vision and Knowledge." *JSNT* 56:53-71.

Himmelfarb, Martha. 1993. *Ascents into Heaven in Jewish and Christian Apocalypses*. Oxford: Oxford University Press.

Hultgren, Arland J. 1987. *Christ and His Benefits: Christology and Redemption in the New Testament*. Philadelphia: Fortress.

Lincoln, Andrew T. 1987. "The Church and Israel in Ephesians 2." *CBQ* 49:605-24.

———. 1995. " 'Stand, therefore . . .': Ephesians 6:10-20 as *Peroratio*." *Biblical Interpretation* 3:99-114.

Lincoln, Andrew T. and A. J. M. Wedderburn. 1993. *The Theology of the Later Pauline Letters*. Cambridge: Cambridge University Press.

Lindemann, Andreas. 1975. *Die Aufhebung der Zeit: Geschichtsverständnis und Eschatologie im Epheserbrief*. Gütersloh: Gerd Mohn.

Long, A. A. and D. N. Sedley. 1987. *The Hellenistic Philosophers*. Vol. 1, *Translations*. Cambridge: Cambridge University Press.

MacDonald, Dennis R. 1987. *There Is No Male and Female: The Fate of a Dominical Saying in Paul and Gnosticism*. HDR 20. Philadelpha: Fortress.

Malherbe, Abraham J. 1977. *The Cynic Epistles*. SBLSBS 12. Missoula, MT: Scholars Press.

———. 1983. "Antisthenes and Odysseus, and Paul at War," *Harvard Theological Review* 76:143-73.

———. 1986. *Moral Exhortation: A Greco-Roman Sourcebook*. Philadelphia: Westminster.

———. 1992. "Hellenistic Moralists and the New Testament." In *Aufstieg und Niedergang der römischen Welt* II 26/1, edited by Wolfgang Haase, 267-333. Berlin: DeGruyter.

Meade, David G. 1986. *Pseudonymity and Canon: An Investigation into the Relationship of Authorship and Authority in the Jewish and Earliest Christian Tradition*. WUNT 39. Tübingen: Mohr-Siebeck.

Meyer, Regina Pacis. 1977. *Kirche und Mission im Epheserbrief*. Stuttgarter Bibelstudien 86. Stuttgart: Katholisches Bibelwerk.

Philo. 1948. *Philo's Works*. 10 volumes. Translated by F. H. Colson. Cambridge, MA: Harvard University Press.

Porter, Stanley E. 1990. "*iste ginōskontes* in Ephesians 5,5: Does Chiasm Solve a Problem?" *ZNW* 81:270-76.

Rapske, Brian. 1994. *The Book of Acts in Its First Century Setting*. Vol. 3, *The Book of Acts and Paul in Roman Custody*. Grand Rapids, MI: Eerdmans.

Robinson, James M., ed. 1988. *The Nag Hammadi Library in English*. Revised ed. San Francisco: Harper & Row.

Sampley, Paul J. 1971. *"And the Two Shall Become One Flesh": A Study of Traditions in Eph 5:21-33*. SNTSMS 16. Cambridge: Cambridge University Press.

Sanders, Jack T. 1993. *Schismatics, Sectarians, Dissidents, Deviants: The First One Hundred Years of Jewish-Christian Relations*. Valley Forge, PA: Trinity Press International.

Schoeni, Marc. 1993. "The Hyperbolic Sublime as a Master Trope in Romans." In *Rhetoric and the New Testament: Essays from the 1992 Heidelberg Conference,* edited by Stanley E. Porter and Thomas H. Olbricht, 71-92. JSNTSup 90. Sheffield: JSOT.

Spicq, Ceslas. 1994. *Theological Lexicon of the New Testament.* 3 vols. Translated by James Ernest. Peabody, MA: Hendrickson.

Trebilco, Paul R. 1991. *Jewish Communities in Asia Minor.* SNTSMS 69. Cambridge: Cambridge University Press.

Trobisch, David. 1994. *Paul's Letter Collection: Tracing the Origins.* Minneapolis: Fortress.

Usami, Kōshi. 1983. *Somatic Comprehension of Unity: The Church in Ephesus.* AnBib 101. Rome: Biblical Institute Press.

White, John L. 1986. *Light from Ancient Letters.* Philadelphia: Fortress.

Wild, Robert A. 1984. "The Warrior and the Prisoner: Some Reflections on Ephesians 6:10-20." *CBQ* 46:284-98.

Wilhelmi, Gerhard. 1987. "Der Versöhner-Hymnus in Eph 2,14ff." *ZNW* 78:145-52.

Wright, M. R. 1995. *Cosmology in Antiquity.* New York: Routledge.

Yarbrough, O. Larry. 1995. "Parents and Children in the Letters of Paul." In *The Social World of the First Christians: Essays in Honor of Wayne A. Meeks.* Edited by L. Michael White and Larry Yarbough, 126-41. Minneapolis: Fortress.

Yorke, L. O. R. 1991. *The Church as the Body of Christ in the Pauline Corpus: A Re-examination.* Lanham, MD: University Press of America.

COMMENTARIES (BOTH CITED AND NOT CITED)

Barth, Markus. 1974. *Ephesians.* 2 vols. AB 34; 34A. Garden City, NY: Doubleday. — Sees Ephesians as written by Paul during his Roman imprisonment. Departures from the language of the undisputed Pauline Epistles are due to extensive use of liturgical material. Provides extended comparison of Ephesians with other Pauline letters.

Bouttier, Chantel. 1991. *L'Épître de Saint Paul aux Éphésiens.* Commentaire du Nouveau Testament deuxième série Ixb. Geneva: Labor et Fides. — Treats the language of Ephesians as a complex poetic structure that draws on a variety of sources. Concludes with excurses on theological topics in Ephesians.

Conzelmann, Hans. 1985. "Der Brief an die Epheser." In *Die Briefe an die Galater, Epheser, Philipper, Kolosser, Thessalonicher und Philemon,* edited by Jürgen Becker, Hans Conzelmann, and Gerhard Friedrich. Göttingen/Zürich: Vandenhoeck & Ruprecht. — An introduction followed by an essay style that comments on the Epistle section by section. Treats Ephesians as a development of the Pauline traditions, especially Colossians, to counter the influence of gnosticizing Christianity. Ephesians takes the cosmological image of the body of Christ as the foundation for a cosmic ecclesiology.

Dibelius, Martin, and D. Heinrich Greeven. 1953. *An die Kolosser, Epheser, an Philemon.* HNT 12. Tübingen: Mohr-Siebeck. — Brief comments on the

Greek text summarize German scholarship in the mid-twentieth century; useful parallels to classical and early Christian literature.

Gnilka, Joachim. 1980. *Der Epheserbrief.* HTKNT. Freiburg: Herder & Herder. — Sees Ephesians as the product of a Pauline school associated with Ephesus that has expanded Paul's thought with both apocalyptic material similar to Qumran and the speculative traditions of the hellenistic synagogue similar to Philo.

Kitchen, Martin. 1994. *Ephesians.* London/New York: Routledge. — More a series of essays on reading Ephesians than a commentary. Contains a helpful discussion of the use of pseudepigraphy in preserving ancient religious traditions. Focuses on Ephesians as a post-70 CE summing up of the Pauline legacy. Hence the thematic discussion of sections of the Epistle begins with Eph. 3. Kitchen thinks that Eph 2:14 interprets the destruction of the Jerusalem temple as evidence that God intends to unite Jew and Gentile.

Lincoln, Andrew T. 1990. *Ephesians.* WBC 42. Dallas: Word. — A major resource for the study of Ephesians. Provides detailed analysis of the Greek text, which is informed by study of ancient rhetorical tradition. Readers without Greek can follow the theological explanations that conclude each section of the commentary.

Martin, Ralph P. 1991. *Ephesians, Colossians and Philemon.* Atlanta: John Knox. — Comments on sections of the letter for the general reader. Treats Ephesians as an encyclical letter to churches in Asia Minor written by a later Pauline disciple against gnosticizing tendencies in the region. Emphasizes the importance of liturgical and baptismal echoes in establishing the believer's claim to share in the victory of the exalted Christ. Concludes each section with suggestions for pastors and teachers.

Mussner, Franz. 1982. *Der Brief an die Epheser.* Gütersloh: Gerd Mohn. — Highlights the influence of Jewish cultic imagery and liturgical language on Ephesians. Sees the letter as addressed to converts who have not yet shed concepts of divinity or behavior typical of their pagan past.

Schlier, Heinrich. 1957. *Der Brief an die Epheser.* Dusseldorf: Patmos. — Provides major excurses on key linguistic terms in Ephesians. Sees the letter as Paul's rejoinder to Jewish Gnostic opponents. Argues that the apostle adopts Gnostic terminology to expound his own theology.

Schnackenburg, Rudolf. 1991. *The Epistle to the Ephesians.* Translated by H. Heron. Edinburgh: T & T Clark. — Translation of a major German commentary published in 1982. Particularly helpful analysis of the logical flow of the letter exhibited in the layout of the author's translation. Concludes with extended discussion of the theological impact of Ephesians in classical Catholic and Protestant views of predestination, Christ and redemption, church, and Christian life.

INDEX